The Waterways of Britain

The Waterways of Britain

A Guide to the Canals and Rivers of England,
Scotland and Wales

Anthony Burton

Photographs by Derek Pratt

WILLOW BOOKS
COLLINS
8 Grafton Street, London
1983

Willow Books
William Collins Sons & Co Ltd
London · Glasgow · Sydney
Auckland · Toronto · Johannesburg

First published in Great Britain 1983

Burton, Anthony
The waterways of Britain
1. Inland navigation – Great Britain
2. Inland and boating – Great Britain
3. Great Britain – Description and
    travel – Guidebooks
I. Title

914.1'04858 DA 650

ISBN 0 00 218047 2

Designed and produced by
Quintet Publishing Limited, London

Editorial Director	Clare Howell
Editor	Janet Law
Art Editor	Christopher White
Designers	Mike Rose Robert Lamb
	Rose & Lamb
	Design Partnership
Illustrations	Sue Rose
Cartography	Oxford Cartographers
	Limited

Phototypeset by
Hugh Wilson Typesetting, Norwich

Illustrations originated by
East Anglian Engraving Limited,
Norwich

Printed and bound in Italy by
Sagdos, Milan

Contents

Introduction

Like millions of others I have always enjoyed 'mucking about in boats' – sailing, canoeing and discovering other aspects of the boating life, such as capsizing and sinking. Yet, for a long time, I never thought of the waterways as such, never considered them as a connected system of natural rivers, linked by unnatural canals. That changed some twenty years ago when, encouraged by friends' stories of a successful holiday, my wife and I took to the canals. We hired a minute fibre-glass cruiser with an outboard motor from the old British Waterways Board hire base at Middlewich and set out for Llangollen. We wrestled with the unfamiliar paddle gear at locks, heaved up lift bridges and discovered the thrills of the mighty Pontcysyllte. We also began a love affair with the canals that has lasted ever since. For the journey added a new dimension to my enjoyment of the water – it introduced this notion of a great transport network all but forgotten and abandoned by the modern world of commerce. It scarcely seemed credible at the time, but had we changed direction – and had we had the time to spare – we could have gone not just to Llangollen but to London, to Birmingham or Manchester. We could have turned away from the Welsh hills for the Pennine hills or the flat expanses of the Fens. We had found not one waterway, but a whole world to explore.

A lot has happened to the British waterways in the last twenty years: old routes have been reopened, more and more hire boats have become available and very many more people have turned to the canals and rivers for their holidays. The newcomer to the system is now faced with a bewildering choice of routes and boats, and one aim of this book is to help make sense out of the complexities. I have also tried to do something else: I have tried to convey something of the special pleasures of waterway travel. For me, this has always been more than the fascination with the routes themselves. Every single time I have stepped on board a narrow boat for another journey, the cares of the world have begun to slip away as if they had been left behind, parked with the car on the steadily receding bank. My hope is that this book will help others to find as much pleasure as I have found over the years in the waterways of Britain.

Anthony Burton

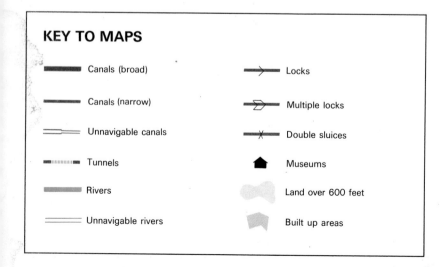

KEY TO MAPS

Canals (broad)	Locks
Canals (narrow)	Multiple locks
Unnavigable canals	Double sluices
Tunnels	Museums
Rivers	Land over 600 feet
Unnavigable rivers	Built up areas

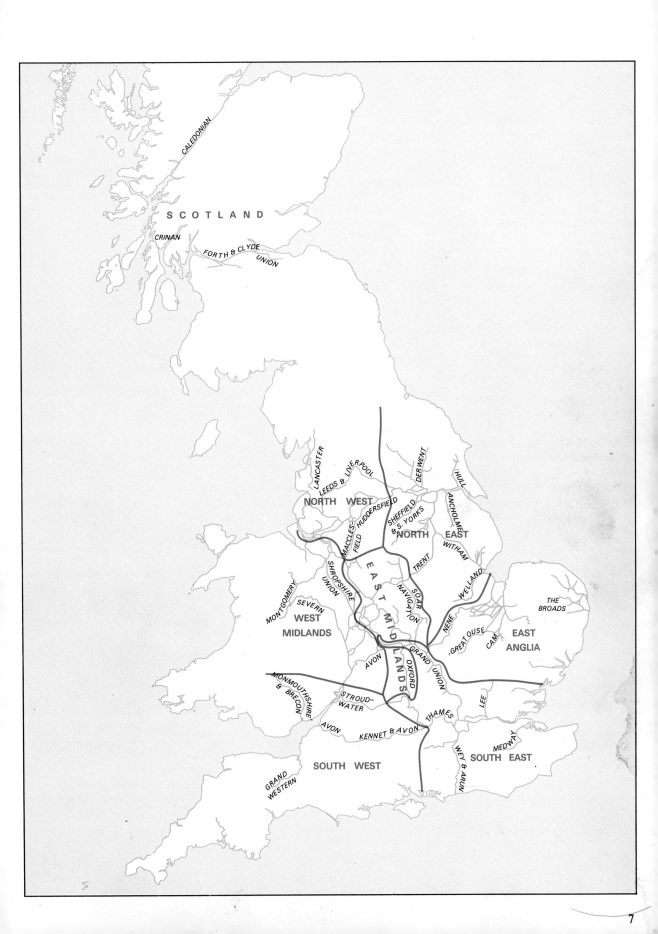

CALEDONIAN

SCOTLAND

CRINAN

FORTH & CLYDE
UNION

LANCASTER

LEEDS & LIVERPOOL

DERWENT

HULL

NORTH WEST

MACCLESFIELD

HUDDERSFIELD

SHEFFIELD
& S. YORKS

ANCHOLME

NORTH EAST

WITHAM

MONTGOMERY

SHROPSHIRE UNION

SEVERN

TRENT

EAST MIDLANDS

SOAR NAVIGATION

NENE

WELLAND

THE BROADS

WEST MIDLANDS

GREAT OUSE

CAM

EAST ANGLIA

AVON

OXFORD

GRAND UNION

MONMOUTHSHIRE & BRECON

STROUD-WATER

THAMES

LEE

AVON

KENNET & AVON

MEDWAY

WEY & ARUN

SOUTH EAST

GRAND WESTERN

SOUTH WEST

The History of the Waterway System

If you could order up a bright summer day and in it view all the 3000 and more miles of Britain's navigable waterways, you would find a scene of infinite variety. You would see the estuaries and tidal rivers as brightly spattered with coloured sails as a confettied churchyard after a wedding. You would find the great rivers no less busy, crowded not with sail but with motor cruisers cheerily churning the waters. And, coming down the watery scale, the narrow canals would be discovered, following their own secretive routes, sidling around the backs of townships or threading a passage through the peaceful countryside. You would even find, among all the pleasure seekers, some who had come to the water to work, for in certain regions there is still a busy trade in goods and cargoes. It might all be thought to add up

to what the travel brochures call 'the unchanging scene', a world 'untouched by time'. Nothing could be further from the reality of the world of the waterways.

If one were to go back in time to the middle of the nineteenth century, the view over the British waterways system would look very different indeed. For a start, there would be far more miles of navigable river and canal than there are today but, much more importantly, there would be virtually no pleasure boats at all. The waterways would be crowded with as great a variety of boats as they are now, but they would be working boats, carrying cargo and passengers. The 'unchanging' world of the waterways that we travel today is the product of a long and complex evolutionary process, a process in which very little thought was given to the wishes of the

pleasure boater, a process designed to serve industry and to make profits. The miracle is that, in pursuing that end, the men who built up the waterway system left us such a magnificently rich heritage, which offers so much enjoyment to so many people. But if we are to understand anything of the special nature and character of the waterway system, to have any inkling of how it achieved its splendid diversity, then we must know a little more about that long period of evolution.

River Trade

No one can say precisely when Britain's rivers were first used for trade, for such use goes back beyond written records, but we do know that by medieval times river traffic was well established. Just as men spoke of the King's High

Road, so the great River Severn was known as the King's High Stream. In the earliest times, rivers were left untouched, but it was not long before men began to tamper with the natural flowing stream. Some of the alterations were made to improve navigation, others to cope with the needs of other river users, for boatmen were by no means the only ones who turned to the rivers for their livelihood. Among those who tampered with the natural order of things were the millers who constructed weirs across the rivers to build up a depth of water on the upstream side, so that part of that water could be diverted to turn their waterwheels. Boats and weirs do not, in the normal way of things, mix very well. On the other hand, the idea of controlling the river, providing deep smooth water above the weirs, was very attractive to the boatmen, if only they could contrive a way of getting the boat across the weir. The method most commonly used was the flash lock. In effect, part of the weir was constructed out of movable wooden boards, and once these were removed the water tumbled through in a great rush or flash, taking the boats along on the flood. This was fine enough for those going downstream who got a free, if somewhat precarious, ride, but meant hard work for the travellers passing upstream who had to haul or winch their vessels against the current. A much more satisfactory method of dealing with changes in the level of the river came with the introduction of the pound lock, the invention of which is generally credited to Leonardo da Vinci. It was introduced into Britain in the sixteenth century yet, surprisingly, the last flash lock did not disappear from the Thames until the present century.

The pound lock gets its name from the fact that it is an enclosed lock, just as the village pound was the enclosure once used to pen sheep and cattle. The typical pound lock is a long, deep chamber closed at either end by stout wooden gates, but supplied with some method of allowing water to get into the lock and out again. This is either through holes cut in the gate and then covered by movable wooden boards (gate paddles), or through culverts, again covered by movable boards (ground paddles).

Left A pair of Fellows, Morton and Clayton narrow boats: the steamer pulling the butty. The white shirts worn by the men were a standard F.M.C. uniform.

Nowadays, we seldom use the expression 'pound lock' and simply talk about locks, the word 'pound' being reserved for the section of the canal between two locks. No one can travel the waterways for long without meeting such devices, which have played a major part in river improvement and canal construction. The use of the pound lock brought a new approach to river improvement. The engineer could still build his weir, easing the river down on its way to the sea through a series of controlled steps, rather than letting it tumble along as it pleased, but now the boatman could be supplied with his very own watery staircase. An artificial cutting was made alongside the natural river to bypass the weir, and the lock was built in the cutting. This system was first used to help ships bypass the shoals and shallows of the River Exe on their way up to Exeter, in the Exeter Canal built between 1564 and 1567. The system spread throughout the seventeenth and early eighteenth centuries, when there was a spate of river improvements. And this is the system that we can still travel today. True, there have been changes in detail – locks have been enlarged, mechanisms for moving paddles have been improved and, in some cases, automated – but the fundamentals remain the same.

By the middle of the eighteenth century, river improvement had been pushed about as far as it could go. There had been major schemes involving miles of artificial cutting and many locks, and some of these, such as the Aire & Calder Navigation, remain in use as commercial waterways today. The rivers were busy with trade and with a splendid variety of craft, from big sailing barges to the hundreds of lighters being pushed and pulled in the frenzied bustle of the Thames. But there were still vast areas of the country untouched by waterways, and for such regions transport meant heavy, lumbering carts that were frequently bogged down in the quagmires that passed for roads, or long trains of pack-horses, each animal carrying a load of no more than 300 pounds. And the need for better transport was increasing all the time, for the pace of industrial life was quickening and the demand for bulky items such as coal steadily increasing. A 300-pound load brought in by pack-horse was not going to keep one of the new, giant steam engines going for very long. Trials had shown that if the load could be taken off the horse's back

A mixture of canal and river craft at Limehouse Basin, London.

and put on a barge, then that same horse could haul a load of as much as 50 tons. All that was needed was the water for the boat to float on, and a way of bringing water to inland towns had already been tried and proved in continental Europe and, nearer at hand, in Ireland: the summit level canal.

The earlier British canals, such as the Exeter, had all been, in effect, forms of watery bypasses, following the line of the natural river and drawing water from it. The summit level canal is quite different, for it is an entirely artificial construction, running across the watershed, linking one river system to another and requiring its own independent water supply through devices such as reservoirs. The Newry Canal was just such a canal, linking the river at Newry to Lough Neagh and the coal mines of Tyrone. It was opened in 1742 and the chief engineer, Thomas Steers, came across to England to work on a waterway to join St Helens to the Mersey near Widnes. Officially, it was another river navigation scheme, intended to make the Sankey Brook navigable; in practice, the largest vessel that could ever have navigated the brook would have been a paper boat. Although, strictly speaking, not a summit canal, it was nevertheless the first entirely artificial canal to be constructed in mainland Britain. But it was still thought of as no more than an extension of old ideas, just another way of making an unnavigable river available for trade and it attracted very little general interest. The same could not be said of the next British canal, the brainchild of Francis Egerton, third Duke of Bridgewater.

The Canal Builders

The Duke of Bridgewater was still in his twenties when he took up canal promotion – not quite the activity one expects of an eighteenth-century aristocrat, and certainly not in accord with the image put forward in romantic fiction. Yet the story of the canal is romantic enough, for the young Duke had immersed himself in the serious business of industry in an attempt to forget an unhappy love affair. He left the world of court and courtesans for his coal mines at Worsley near Manchester, and was at once faced with a problem. He had the coal, Manchester wanted the coal – but how was the coal to be got from one to the other? The answer was to dig a canal, an entirely artificial canal that would run from the very heart of the mines into Manchester. At first he thought of taking it no further than the River Irwell, but the Irwell Navigation authorities, believing that they had the whip hand, made outrageous demands in terms of high tolls. So the Duke, working in collaboration with his agent, John Gilbert, and a millwright from Derbyshire, James Brindley, took a bold decision. If the Irwell authorities would not let the Bridgewater Canal join the river, then the canal would ignore it by simply leaping over it. And that is precisely what happened: the canal was carried over the river at Barton on an aqueduct.

The Sankey Brook had seemed to be just one more navigation scheme among many, but here was something to catch the popular imagination. Boats in the air, passing over boats underneath – it was the talk of the fashionable world. No lady or gentleman taking Britain's version of the Grand Tour would want to miss this amazing sight, and carriages making their way to the scenic delights of Snowdonia or the Lakes turned aside to take their owners to view the Duke's watery bridge, his canal in the sky. It is difficult now to appreciate the excitement it caused for the old aqueduct itself has gone, knocked down to make way for a new and mightier waterway, the Manchester Ship Canal. But the Duke's canal still takes its airy passage, in a new marvel of the canal age. It is carried across the Ship Canal on a movable aqueduct, which pivots so that it can be swung out to make way for ships on the wider canal below.

The first Barton Aqueduct was the wonder of the age, but among those who made the trip to Lancashire were some who looked at other aspects of the new marvel. The Duke had staked his entire fortune on the venture, and he had won. He had been able to halve the price of his coal on sale in Manchester, and the profits were rolling in. The Duke's bank balance was of more interest to some than the Duke's aqueduct. Industrialists in the land-locked heart of England began to dream of a new, improved transport system; speculators began to dream of new and increased profits.

Both were to play their part in financing the canal age, which reached its peak at the end of the eighteenth century; in three remarkable years from 1792 to 1795, Parliament authorized the construction of no less than 36 new canals in England, Scotland and Wales.

It is against this background that we must see the waterways of today. The canals and river navigations developed to meet specific needs and particular interests. Sometimes those interests worked together, sometimes they were in conflict. It is because of this diversity that we have a system in which no two parts are ever quite the same. The diversity had its origins in the regional craft that used the rivers and estuaries and which traded around the British coast. As the canal system spread outwards from the older river system, so it was adapted to accommodate the craft already in use. When the Duke of Bridgewater laid plans to extend his canal southwards to the Mersey, he had the firm intention of building it in such a

way that it would take the traditional craft of the Mersey, the Mersey flats. The absolute limiting factor on boats using a waterway is the size of the locks: if the boat will not fit the lock then it cannot use the waterway. Trading flats were sailing barges roughly 70 feet long by 14 feet wide, so the locks at Runcorn, joining the canal to the river, were built to take such boats. In time, the Duke built up his own fleet of flats which became known as 'dukers'. Across on the other side of the country, in Yorkshire, the traditional trading barges were the Humber keels, with their great square sails, and waterways such as the Aire &

Below The old and the new: a boat is laboriously rowed on the Irwell Navigation, while a barge passes above on the Bridgewater Canal's Barton Aqueduct.

Right The grand opening of Marple Aqueduct on the Peak Forest Canal.

Calder and the Sheffield Canal were built to accommodate them. So it was that, in many areas, local interests and local practices determined the size and nature of the waterways, with scant attention being paid to any possible connections between waterways. But, when it came to the new generation of artificial canals threading their way through the Midlands, new factors came into play. Canals of a very different character were built.

Following the success of the Bridgewater Canal, there was a sudden rush of new canal schemes. But the promoters of the new canals faced a difficulty. Who was to build them? The obvious candidates were the triumvirate who had supervised the Bridgewater; but the Duke had his own affairs to tend, Gilbert was committed to the Duke, so that left just one man, the millwright James Brindley. There was scarcely a canal scheme in the early years in which Brindley did not have a hand, and it was the decisions taken by him in those first decades which set the pattern for an important part of the British canal system.

The first and most important decision came when he set the size of locks for the new generation of waterways. In his work at Runcorn he had had little choice, but when he arrived in the Midlands he was concerned with building up an interlocking system, in every sense of the word. In 1766, work began on two new canals: the Staffordshire & Worcestershire and the Trent & Mersey. They were part of this connected system, so that decisions taken on one would affect the other, as well as later canals built in the same region. There were two problems worrying Brindley. The first was how to ensure a sufficient water supply for his new canal. With a lock-free canal this was no great problem. Fill it up with water and the water will more or less stay there, apart from a certain amount of evaporation – assuming, of course, that you can stop it draining away through the bottom of the canal. Brindley had solved the problem of making his canals watertight by the introduction of 'puddle', a gooey mixture of clay, sand and water stomped into the canal bed by the heavy boots of the navvies. Incidentally, the name 'navvy' itself originated on the canal system as an abbreviation of 'navigator', a man working on a navigation. With a summit canal, however, water supply represented more of a problem. Coming downhill, the boat enters the lock, then as the boat descends the water runs out at the bottom of the lock. That lock-full of water passes on down to the next lock and so on until eventually it reaches another canal or river and joins the outward flow to the sea. Every boat crossing the summit uses at least two lock-fulls of water; one going up and one coming down. A boat using a Runcorn-sized lock with a fall of, say, six feet would be pushing out nearly 40,000 gallons of water: double that for a boat crossing the summit and you have the daunting figure of 80,000 gallons per

boat. That meant 80,000 gallons had to be replaced from somewhere.

The second problem was even more of a worry. On the Trent & Mersey Canal he was faced by the long, tall ridge of Harecastle Hill to the north of Stoke-on-Trent. It was too high to go over and too long to go round, so Brindley went through it by tunnel. He had no precedents to guide him, for transport tunnels were an unknown quantity in Britain. Here was something else to worry about: how wide could he make the tunnel? The problem was related to the lock problem: the locks, he felt, should not be too big, nor should the tunnel be too wide. As there was no point in having a lock wider than the tunnel, he took the decision to halve the width of the locks he had used at Runcorn. His new locks would still be a little over 70 feet long, but just over seven feet wide – and his tunnel could be kept to the same width. As it was, the tunnel proved immensely difficult and it took 11 years to complete, by which time Brindley was dead.

Now the standard had been set which was to dominate the British canal scene. Special narrow boats were built to fit Brindley's new narrow locks and these became the vessels which were to typify British canals. Thousand upon thousand of narrow boats were built, pulled over the still waters by patient horses trudging along the towpath. Later the horse was replaced by the steam and then the petrol and diesel engine, but the overall shape of the boat remained much the same. That same shape can still be seen in the few surviving working boats and in the huge fleet of hire boats which have adapted that basic design to the holiday trade.

Canals of the Brindley age – and Brindley so dominated the early years that no other name is conceivable – have one other special characteristic. It is a characteristic much appreciated by holiday makers, but one which was a source of great irritation to the working boatmen: they meander. Brindley's inclination when faced by an obstacle such as a hill was not to go through it or over it but, wherever possible, to go round it. This technique, known as contour cutting because the canal follows the natural contours of the land, is the hallmark of the Brindley canal. It can be seen, for example, on the Staffordshire & Worcestershire and the southern section of the Oxford – both canals which derive a good deal of their charm

from Brindley's wayward line. Take this wandering route and add the small-scale pleasures of these early canals – the steady spattering of narrow locks, the mellow high-arched bridges, the small wharves and warehouses – and one can see why so many people now turn to the Brindley canals. It is difficult to imagine them as they once were – the great commercial arteries of the nation.

After Brindley's death a new generation of canal engineers appeared with new ideas, men such as William Jessop, John Rennie and Thomas Telford. With growing expertise in the techniques of construction they could take far bolder decisions when planning a new canal. The hill which would have sent one of the first generation of engineers off on a ramble round the countryside, was now cut open and the canal forced through the middle in a deep cutting. Valleys were crossed on high aqueducts, cul-

Above Portrait of Thomas Telford seated in front of the Pontcysyllte Aqueduct.

Right Narrow boat decoration still flourishes. Here the traditional roses are being painted on a Buckby can.

minating in the mighty Pontcysyllte which carried what was then known as the Ellesmere Canal across the Dee near Llangollen. If the contour canal epitomized the first age, then Pontcysyllte is the emblem of the second. Here industrial revolution technology can be seen at work in the iron trough carrying vessels 120 feet above the waters of the Dee.

Some might look at the later canals and mourn the passing of the picturesque charm of the older routes: but that loss is amply compensated for by the drama of the new. A canal such as the Shropshire

Union, completed at the very end of the canal age, is a canal of straight lines, but straight lines only made possible by superb feats of civil engineering. Deep, leafy cuttings carve through the hills while no less spectacular embankments carry the line high above the valleys.

Within these broad categories of old and new canals there is an infinity of small variations, for no two engineers ever found the same solution to similar problems. Among the delights that come with years of canal travel is the growing recognition of personal styles. One comes to recognize the elegance of Rennie or the architectural quirks of Telford. Yet the whole canal system was built up in a remarkably short time: the Bridgewater was built in 1760 and by the 1830s investors were turning away from canals to the steam railway. It is often said that the railways killed off the British canals, but this is by no means wholly true. Certainly, railway companies bought up many canals, but to run them not to close them, though it must be said that the canals were very much the poor country cousins in the railway household. The days when fortunes could be made on the canals were gone for ever, and the boatmen had to struggle hard against the new competitor. It was

Above Sailing ships on the Caledonian Canal, Corpach.

Right Rebuilding Boulter's Lock on the Thames, 1912.

during the railway age that the boatmen were forced to cut their costs by leaving their homes on land for a permanently nomadic life. Whole families lived in the tiny back cabins of the narrow boats, which were small miracles of organization and were made more tolerable by the traditional bright decoration of roses and castles. This is the popular picture of the boating family but it is, in canal terms, a modern one, for this way of life was virtually unknown until the canal age was into its second century.

It was not the railways that killed the canals, but the motor lorry. Attempts were made to keep the system alive in the years after the Second World War when canals were nationalized along with the railways, but the commercial life was slipping away. Today, there is little narrow boat traffic but there is a comparatively thriving barge traffic on the broad waterways, such as those of the North-East. But a new commercial trade has developed to take the place of the old. Many canals are busier now than they have been for decades, not carrying cargo for industry but carrying people on holiday. They are a source of pleasure and business for an estimated three million each year. It is a tribute to the men who built up the waterway system that it should still be in use today. It is a tribute to the quality of their craftsmanship that it can be appreciated not just for its commercial potential, not just for the way it helped build Britain's industrial wealth, but also for its intrinsic worth. It is the standard of workmanship, of materials and design and, perhaps as much as anything else, the sense of individuality, which have ensured that people return to find the beauty of the waterways. And there is no better way to discover those beauties than to see them as they should be seen, from a boat slowly making its way across the placid waters of our canals and rivers.

Using the Waterways

The three questions most commonly asked by those who are planning a waterways holiday for the first time are: where should I go; what sort of boat should I get; shall I be able to handle the boat once I have it? In many respects, the first question is the most difficult to answer, especially when it comes in the alternative form: which is the best waterway to start on? That question has no answer at all, since it must depend on individual preference, and the most experienced boaters have the greatest difficulty in deciding which is their own personal favourite, let alone advising others. So there can be no clear-cut answer – no way of saying 'the best place to start is so-and-so'. There are, however, a number of ways in which the beginner can reach that crucial decision on where to start – and the same methods are just as useful when deciding where to go to after that.

Planning Your Holiday

The first consideration is the length of time you intend to be away – a weekend, a week, two weeks or whatever. Once you have decided that, you should then be able to work out the distance you can travel in that time, which is not quite the simple matter it might seem. The commonest mistake is to overestimate how far you can get. The brochures will tell you that the speed limit on canals is four m.p.h., though it is greater on rivers. This does not mean that you will necessarily be able to do four miles in an hour, especially if you are unused to handling a boat. There are all kinds of obstacles in the way of steady progress: bridges to be negotiated with care, shallow sections where the boat can never go at the maximum speed and, most importantly, there are locks. The length of time required to go through a lock depends on how long it takes to empty and fill, and on how many people are waiting to use it – a real factor to bear in mind if you are travelling a popular route in the summer holidays. If you are on a canal or river where you work the locks yourself – and this will be the case on nearly all canals – then you will find it slow going until you have worked everything out. If the locks are manned, you may find that lock keepers will wait until they have got as many boats as possible into a lock before they close the gates and open the paddles.

A holiday boat passing working boats on the Leicester Section of the Grand Union.

This list of problems may make it all sound rather tedious. It is not at all and most people enjoy the bustle and interest of lock working – and feel decidedly cheated when there are no locks to work. So, given all those factors, how on earth do you begin to work out how far you can go? A useful measurement is the lock-mile: count each lock as being the equivalent of an extra half-mile of waterway. So that, for example, the Peak Forest Canal which is 15 miles long and has 16 locks works out at 23 lock-miles. If you allow yourself an average speed of three m.p.h. this gives a time factor of roughly eight hours.

It is up to individuals to decide how many hours a day they want to spend actually travelling in the boat, but ask the majority of those who love the waterways and come back year after year, and they will say the same thing – *don't hurry.*

Canal and river travel offer peace and relaxation – a way of slowing down the pace of life, of taking time really to see the world about us. So, in planning a route it is always a good rule to underestimate rather than overestimate the distance you will travel. Set yourself too ambitious a goal and you will be rushing to get there, and feel frustrated if you fail.

Allow plenty of time, and the worst that can happen is that you will find yourself with time in hand to explore further than you intended.

Having got some idea of how far you might travel, there is still the real problem of where to go. Many people are attracted by the idea of 'rings' such as the Cheshire Ring and the Avon Ring, routes which allow for a circular trip. Circular routes are fine in many ways, but it is all too easy to fall into the trap of being over-ambitious. The Cheshire Ring, for example (along the Macclesfield to the Peak Forest, down through Manchester and out on the

Bridgewater to the Trent & Mersey to complete the circle), can be done in one week – but it most certainly cannot be done comfortably in one week. And, once embarked on a ring, the traveller feels compelled to push on to the end and has, of course, to get back to the hire base. Far better to allow two weeks and then, if you have time in hand, simply potter on to somewhere else as a bonus.

Left Peace and quiet on the Llangollen Canal near Trevor.

Below Bunbury locks where the old stables for the work horses still survive.

Rings are popular largely because people have the notion that it must be very tedious to go up a route and then turn round and come back again. Happily, this is not so in practice. Coming back over the route you travelled just a few days before, you are constantly amazed by how different everything seems simply because you are travelling in the opposite direction. And such routes have this great advantage: you have no need to set yourself goals. Simply cast off on the waterway of your choice, travel on at the pace that suits you and when you are halfway through your allotted time, turn round and come

back again. Do, however, make sure there is a spot where you can turn. Canals are too narrow for most boats to turn in, so special 'winding holes' are provided where you can make the manoeuvre. It is also as well to remember if you are travelling on a river that you will move faster with the current than you will against it.

The actual choice of waterway will depend on what you are looking for in the holiday. Some of you will want rural peace and quiet; others will like the idea of using the waterway to visit interesting towns; while some will want spectacular features such as high aqueducts. The

only thing to be done is to find out as much as you can about the various waterways to see which sounds most likely to meet your particular needs. The gazetteer that follows is designed to help with this task. The beginner would, however, be well advised to keep clear of all tidal waters, which should never be tackled by the inexperienced.

Hiring Your Boat

Having chosen the waterway, there comes the question of choosing the boat. I am making two assumptions: the first is that the beginner will be hiring rather than buying, and the second is that the boat will be a motor boat. There are areas such as the Norfolk Broads where it is possible – and, many would argue, preferable – to sail, but sailing boats would require a separate book.

The first-time hirer is faced by a bewildering array of hire companies and hire boats, and that first choice can be very important. Many have started out badly and simply turned away from the waterways for ever. No one can guarantee a successful holiday, given the fickle British climate and the tendency for all mechanical objects to go wrong sometimes, but careful planning can at least minimize the chances of disaster.

Rule number one is that you can never get too much information. There is a number of organizations which offer boats on a variety of waterways, such as Blakes, Hoseasons and Boat Enquiries of Oxford. All produce informative, illustrated brochures. But they do not cover the full range of options. The Inland Waterways Association publishes an annual *Inland Waterways Guide to Holiday Hire,* listing the hire firms on different waterways, while the two principal specialist magazines, *Waterways World* and *Canal and Riverboat Monthly* carry advertisements from a variety of companies. They also publish regular reviews of hire boats and hire companies. Study the adverts, get the brochures from as many companies as you think look likely to meet your needs and check to see exactly what is being offered for the money. Does the boat have a licence for the particular waterway on which you wish to cruise, for example? Is fuel included in the cost? Then if possible go and see the boats for yourself. Do not worry about people who tell you that there is a 'proper boat' for the canals. The proper boat is the one in which you enjoy yourself and have a first-class holiday.

Above A pair of working boats now adapted for use for the new holiday trade.

Right Entering Salters Lode Lock on the Middle Level.

Steering can be either by wheel or by tiller. Many of us start off on the water knowing how to steer a car, but with little notion of how to handle a boat, so we tend to go for the boats where the 'driver' sits at the front with a steering-wheel in his or her hand. Unfortunately, there is not much similarity between boats and cars – indeed, they could be said to work in precisely opposite ways. Turn the steering-wheel of the car and the front wheels move and the rest of the car follows; turn the wheel of a boat and the effect is felt at the stern not in the bows. This means that boats with forward steering positions are quite difficult to handle, since all the action is going on behind the steerer's back. In general, a long boat is much easier to steer from the stern than from the bows. The relative merits of steering-wheel and tiller are less easily established. The tiller has the advantage of having a very positive, direct action, but the novice is often initially put off by the fact that you have to push the tiller one way in order to go in the opposite direction. In practice, it is a skill soon learned, though the finer skills of steering take somewhat longer to acquire. With a steering-wheel, that particular problem ceases to exist, but new problems appear, for the steering-wheel of a boat does not produce the immediate response that one gets from a car. Each form of steering has its enthusiasts, though the majority probably favour tiller steering for traditional canal craft.

The next choice is the type of craft, and again there is no hard and fast rule, but for canal travel the steel-hulled narrow boat offers several advantages. It is robust, manageable and, being developed from the old working narrow boats, particularly well adapted to this type of cruising. It has the advantage over fibreglass in that, being heavy, it sits more solidly in the water, and is less liable to skitter over it in a high wind. With river craft, different criteria often apply. In deep, fast-running rivers there are advantages in having a deeper-keeled boat and for waterways such as the Caledonian Canal, linking together wide canal and the open waters of big lochs, something altogether more seaworthy is required. In the end, the individual has to take the decision, but it is as well to look at as many different craft as possible first. Study brochures, make a

short list and, if possible, call in at the boatyard yourself: most boatyards are only too happy to show off their wares to potential customers.

Boat Handling

You have chosen your waterway, selected the boat and the day arrives when the holiday begins: you are about to take charge. The boatyard staff will wave goodbye and you will be on your own. The better boatyards will make a real effort to show you what is what before handing over command, but the lesson will necessarily be brief. Boat handling on rivers and canals is not essentially difficult – but it is difficult to do well. Expert boat handling can only come with experience, and all too often the beginner is sent on his or her way without even the bare minimum of knowledge required for competence. There is no real substitute for practical experience, but nevertheless a few simple rules can be learned in advance, and they will help to make the real learning process that much easier.

All hire companies will take some time to show you the basic controls. Most will also take the beginners out for a short trip before sending them on their way, but the amount of time given to instruction will vary enormously. I shall assume that you know nothing whatsoever. So, there you are, faced by anything up to 70 feet of boat and you are in charge. The first task is to get away from the moorings, so start the engines and bring mooring spikes and mooring lines back on board. This might sound blindingly obvious, but it is not unknown in that first moment for a crew to untie the lines on the boat and chug off into the distance with no means of ever mooring up again. So, bring the lines aboard and coil them immediately, starting the coils at the end fastened to the boat. This is one of those rules which should always be followed, not just because you want to keep the boat neat and tidy, but for good, sound practical reasons. A tangled rope is a dangerous rope, inviting you to trip over it, and any rope that is not properly coiled will somehow manage to get itself into an unholy tangle. Time and again you will see a crew who need to get a line ashore pick up one of those tangles, heave it away, only to see the rope land with an embarrassing plop in the water between boat and bank.

If your boat is tied to a wharf, then you probably have deep water beneath your keel and you can simply put the engine

into forward gear and steer away from the side. On other moorings, the chances are that you will have very little water beneath the keel, because you will be tied to a muddy bank. Because the driving force for your boat is the propellor at the stern, if you shove the bows out, the stern will move towards the bank and go aground. The simplest method of getting away is to pull up the mooring spikes, get the crew on board with the lines and then, checking first to see that there are no other boats coming along, push the stern away from the bank. Put the engine into reverse and take the boat out into midstream. Once there you can safely engage forward gear and set off on your way. You will soon find that you gain confidence in steering a straight line, though it might not seem so at first. The beginner has a tendency to overcorrect, so that progress up the waterway is a zig-zag affair, rather like a tacking yacht. The secret is to correct a movement before it has a chance to develop. If you wait until the boat has swung a long way out of line, you will find yourself swinging back too far the other way. Do not wait until the boat is

Above Opening one of the unusual 'Jack Clough' paddles on the Leeds & Liverpool Canal.

Below Pub sign, St. Neots, on the Great Ouse.

Right Negotiating Bumblehole Bridge on the Staffordshire & Worcestershire Canal.

facing precisely the way you want it before you move the tiller or wheel back to centre. That will be too late, and your boat will already be setting off on a new direction, and need correcting again.

You may find yourself faced with problems almost immediately, such as boats coming towards you. The rule of the water road is that boats should pass port to port or, in lay terms, if you see a boat coming towards you slow down and move to the right. You must remember, however, that a boat can only be controlled if a certain minimum speed is maintained. Bridges present another test of steering skill. On rivers the gaps between arches may look enormous, but caution is still necessary as the flow of water round a bridge can be tricky. Canal bridges alarm by the comparative narrowness of the opening. In fact, the one thing you can be quite sure about is that there is, in spite of appearances, plenty of room and thousands of boats as wide as yours have gone quite happily through. Slow down and line up your boat well in advance. Do not aim for the centre of the arch; it does not come above the centre of the channel, since most bridges have towpaths underneath. Steer instead to allow a gap of about a foot between the side of the boat and the towpath and the other side will look after itself. Keep the boat straight until the stern is clear and then speed up again. It really is as simple as that.

It is an extremely good idea, as soon as you reach a nice quiet section of waterway, to try stopping your boat. A boat does not come equipped with a set of brakes. It is stopped by putting the engine into reverse. Trying this to see how long it takes and how it works before you need to stop in an emergency is only common sense. Stopping is obviously something you will need to do at some time, possibly even when you reach your very first lock.

How to work a lock

River locks and canal locks are generally quite different, in that the former are frequently operated by professional lock keepers, while canal locks are strictly do-it-yourself. Lock keepers are absolute rulers of their domain. They will tell you just what to do and their instructions must be followed exactly. We shall start, however, by looking at the canal lock.

As a general rule, you will need someone on the boat and at least one other person on the bank to work a lock. As you cannot enter a lock until it is set, it is a good idea to land the shore party in advance. Keep an eye on the canal map, and when the lock is near set the lock party ashore. Quite the easiest way to do this is to let them step off at the bridge before the lock, making sure that they take the windlasses to work the lock with them. If you are travelling uphill, the lock needs to be empty before the boat can enter, and full if you are travelling downhill. Sod's Law dictates that it will usually be the wrong way round. So, let us assume that you wish to go up the lock which, on arrival, turns out to be full of water. Before doing anything else, look to see if there is a boat coming along that could go down the lock. This is not just courtesy but an important way of saving water. If all is clear, check that the paddles on the top (uphill) side are closed, then wind up the paddles on the bottom gates. The boat should stay well clear of the lock as the rush of water causes unpleasant, whirling currents. When the lock is empty, but not before, the gates will open with ease. The boat can now go, steadily and slowly, into the lock – allowing plenty of time to stop. Once completely stopped, it is a good idea to pass a line round one of the lock-side bollards and then back to the boat. Two lines are even better, but that will depend on the number of people on board. Whatever you do, never tie the boat up in a lock, especially when going down, for the water will drop leaving you, quite literally, high and dry. In a wide lock, the lines will prevent you from swinging from side to side and they are still necessary in narrow locks as the flow of water when the paddles are opened sucks the boat forwards. It is possible to use the engine to hold the boat against the flow and, of course, the nearer the boat is to the top gates the less the problem will be. Once your boat is secure inside the lock, the bottom gates can be closed and the paddles lowered by the windlass. They should never be allowed simply to drop under their own weight. The top paddles can now be opened and the lock filled. When the water has reached the top you can open the gates and be on your way, making sure that you have closed the gates and paddles behind you. Going downhill is a similar operation, but in reverse. There is one special point to bear in mind, however: do not get too near the back of the lock. As you can see from the diagram, the top gates rest on a sill, and if the boat catches on that it can tip over. Should that happen or should anything go wrong during locking, never rush around in a panic. Simply close all paddles to stop the water movement as a first step and then assess what needs to be done. In most cases, raising the water level to refloat the boat will be sufficient.

Controlled river locks represent quite

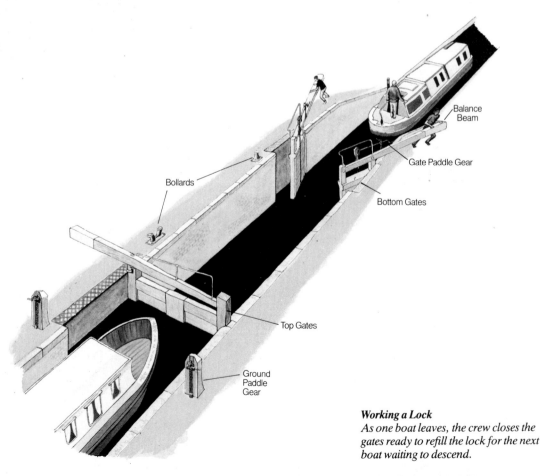

Bollards

Balance Beam

Gate Paddle Gear

Bottom Gates

Top Gates

Ground Paddle Gear

Working a Lock
As one boat leaves, the crew closes the gates ready to refill the lock for the next boat waiting to descend.

a different problem. You must wait until called into the lock by the lock keeper, which frequently involves temporary mooring alongside pilings or in the lock cutting. Be ready to move immediately when asked to do so. Once in the lock you will be given precise instructions: follow those instructions and all will be well. There is, however, one essential in negotiating river locks: do make sure that you are heading towards the lock in the first place, and not over the weir. The navigation channel should be clearly marked, but vandalism is not, alas, unknown. Always keep an eye on the map to make sure you know which way is which. If in doubt, check and double check.

Once you have safely negotiated your first lock and discovered that it is not only simple but fun as well, you can really relax and enjoy yourself. However, there will inevitably be minor crises to face. At some stage you will stem up, the boater's name for running aground. Everybody does it, so there is no cause for embarrassment or alarm. The first thing to do is to put the engine into neutral to stop the boat going even deeper into the mire. Then put the engine into reverse and, with luck, you will come clear. If not, you will have to use a little muscle power, using the boat hook for example, or a pole to push yourself clear. Another common hazard, especially on urban canals, is the fouled propellor – the chief culprit being the ubiquitous polythene bag. You will find that you suddenly lose power, indicating that the propellor is not working properly. Nine times out of ten you can dislodge the obstruction by reversing the engine. On the tenth time, you will have to get your hands wet. Turn off the engine. At the stern of the boat you will find a tightly-fitting weed hatch which when opened allows you to plunge your hands into the water and reach the propellor. Usually the obstruction can be pulled loose, but it is as well to have a pair of pliers with you on the boat to use on the more difficult tangles, such as wire. Once the propellor is free, close and secure the weed hatch. Then, and only then, turn on the engine again.

Boat passing downstream

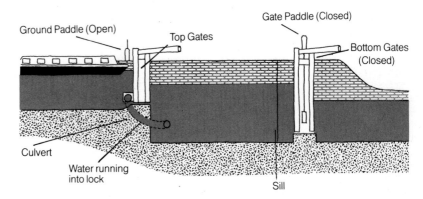

1.   The lock is filling through the open ground paddles. The bottom gates and paddles are closed. The boat waits for the water level to rise.

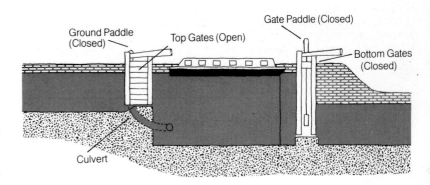

2.   When the water levels are equal, all paddles are closed and the top gates are opened. The boat enters the lock.

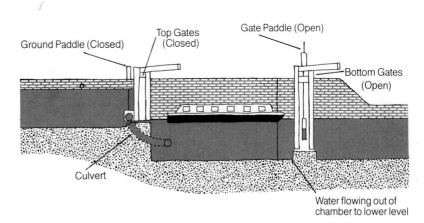

3.   For the boat to descend the lock, the top gates are closed and the bottom gate paddles are opened.

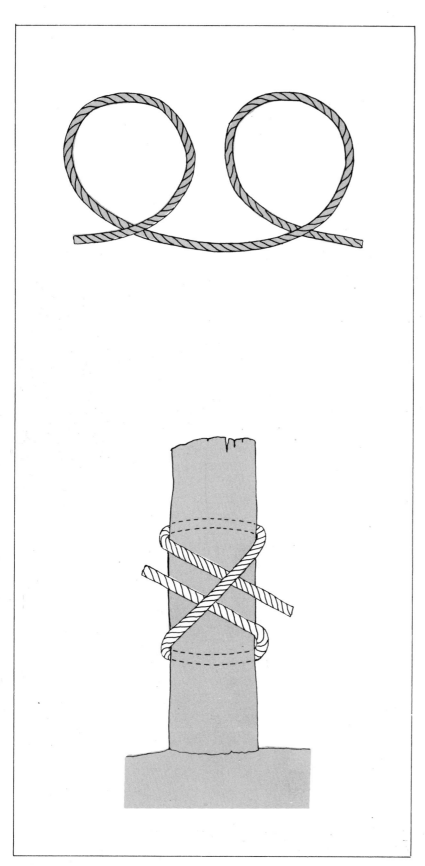

Mooring

Hazards survived, bridges negotiated and locks safely passed, the time will come to moor the vessel. On rivers, mooring is generally limited to specified areas, while on canals the towpath side is generally available, with certain exceptions. Mooring is not permitted near locks or between locks when they are grouped close together to form a flight of locks, and anywhere that is going to make your boat a nuisance to others should be avoided. So do not moor on bends, too close to bridges and so forth. It is just a matter of using common sense. To approach a mooring, the rule as with so many other situations is: take it easy. Edge gently in towards the bank; the water might not be as deep as you think. There will always be those who take death-defying leaps ashore clutching mooring lines. This should not be necessary. Bring the boat in slowly, bows edging into the bank to allow the landing party ashore, taking with them the lines, mooring spikes and hammer. It may sometimes be necessary to throw the stern line ashore and haul on it to bring the boat in, though with practice the engine can be used for the manoeuvre. The ideal mooring is one where the vessel does not grate along the bottom, where lines are set to minimize movement and where lines can pass round the spike or bollard to be fastened back on the boat. Where it is possible to tie up the boat, a simple series of figure-of-eights round the cleats will suffice. If it is necessary to tie up on the shore, then the clove hitch is generally adequate. Bear in mind, however, that river levels can change, so check the moorings at intervals. That done, you can rest easy knowing the boat is secure, and that all those nagging doubts about boat handling have proved quite groundless. You are well on your way to enjoying your boating holiday.

Right Cruising on the Ouse.

The South-East

Any division that one makes in the waterway system of Britain is necessarily somewhat arbitrary. Rivers and canals have the habit of progressing by sometimes long and frequently tortuous routes across country, making classification extremely difficult. It is, nevertheless, convenient to make some attempt at regional division in order to review the whole system in manageable chunks. That way, one can at least decide on a likely boating area and then discover just what that area has to offer. In the case of the South-East, however, the problems are in one sense minimized, since the navigable waterways available for exploration are dominated by two of their number: the River Thames and the Grand Union Canal. These are major trunk routes stretching out from London to the very heart of the Midlands. They are important in every way, both in their roles as historical trade routes and as immensely popular holiday routes. So dominant are they that the other waterways of the region tend to be comparatively neglected. In one sense, this is a positive advantage, since the other routes can offer their own distinct and quiet pleasures. But whether one chooses to travel a popular route, explore some peaceful backwater or go on foot to see one of the routes still being restored to navigation, this region offers a great deal to enjoy.

The Medway

The Thames

The Basingstoke Canal

The Wey & Arun Junction Canal

The Arun

The Wey

The Grand Union Canal

The Lee and Stort

The Chelmer & Blackwater Navigation

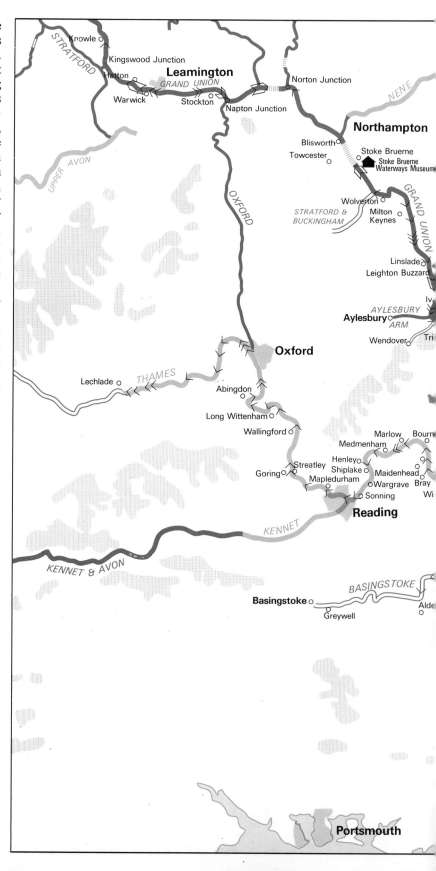

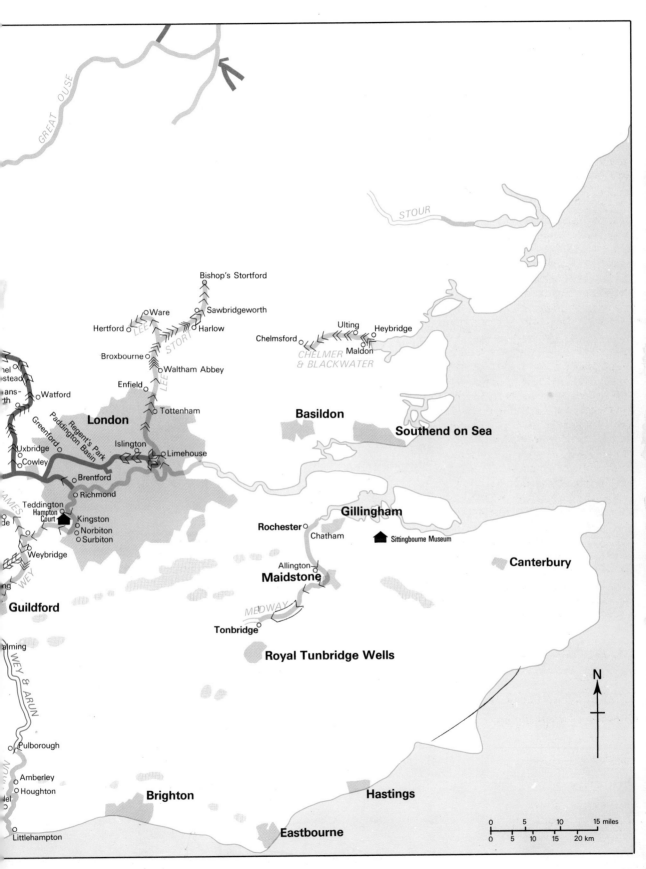

GREAT OUSE

STOUR

Bishop's Stortford

Ware
Sawbridgeworth
Hertford
Harlow

LEE
STORT

Ulting
Heybridge
Chelmsford
Maldon

CHELMER
& BLACKWATER

Broxbourne

Waltham Abbey

Enfield

Tottenham

Basildon

Southend on Sea

hel
stead
ansth

Watford

London

Greenford
Paddington Basin
Regent's Park
Islington

Uxbridge
Cowley

Limehouse

Brentford

Richmond

THAMES

Teddington
Hampton
Court
Kingston
Norbiton
Surbiton

de

WEY

Weybridge

Gillingham

Rochester
Chatham

Sittingbourne Museum

Canterbury

ng

Guildford

Allington

Maidstone

MEDWAY

Tonbridge

Royal Tunbridge Wells

alming

WEY
& ARUN

N

Pulborough

NUN

Amberley
Houghton

Brighton

Hastings

del

Littlehampton

Eastbourne

0	5	10	15 miles
0	5	10	15	20 km

The Medway

The Medway is a river possessed of two quite distinct characters. For 25 miles, from its confluence with the Thames at Sheerness to the sea lock at Allington, it is a tidal river used by a huge variety of craft. Here you can find both the Royal Navy and the Merchant Navy and a rich mixture of sailing craft and large cruisers. Above Allington Lock are another 18 miles of gentle – or, after heavy rain, not so gentle – river, winding off between the hop fields and oast houses of Kent. It is a river which, if it were readily accessible to river boaters would be immensely popular, but which offers instead splendid prospects of peaceful and gentle cruising.

It is possible to reach the Medway from the Thames, but it is not a trip to be undertaken lightly in any but a seaworthy craft.

The waters around Sheerness may officially be part of the estuary, but they can seem more like the North Sea. The river is wide and deep, populated by all kinds of craft, including the lovely sailing barges which race here annually as part of the Thames Sailing Barge Match programme. Moving inland, the river gradually begins to narrow until by the time Chatham is reached it seems to have reached more manageable proportions, though even here great care is needed to keep clear of the busy, commercial shipping.

Rochester is a town dominated by its fine Norman castle and marks the normal limit for the bigger ships. This does not, however, mean that the boatman can now relax, for navigation can still be tricky, especially when the river is high. It remains tidal and troublesome to Allington just below Maidstone. Even when one is safely through the sea lock troubles are by no means necessarily over, for the river tends to rise rapidly in bad weather, and sweeps across weirs in torrents. It remains, throughout its length, a river where great care is needed. For those prepared to exercise that care

it offers, by way of compensation, great rewards. It is a river which takes one to Tonbridge and beyond; deep into the rural heart of Kent. To penetrate that heart, there are 10 locks to be negotiated, and locks quite unlike those on other river navigations, for there are as many as six gate paddles – all very good exercise for the boater. These are fierce in operation, so ropes are very necessary when passing through. The scenery is not dramatic; but serenely beautiful, the river winding round the small hills and wooded valleys. As befits a country so liberally supplied with hop fields and oast houses, there is no shortage of decent inns for the traveller. The Medway offers many delights, but it is not a river that can be fully explored by the inexperienced.

Below Oast houses and the old bridge combine to produce the perfect Medway scene at Teston.

Right Mud flats and moorings at Rochester.

The Thames

The Thames may not be the longest river in Britain but it is certainly the most important and, in terms of holiday makers, far and away the most popular. Cruising is generally limited to the non-tidal reaches above Teddington Lock, the length under the control of the Thames Conservancy. It certainly offers ample scope for holiday makers with 125 miles of navigable waterway and 44 locks. There are, however, occasions when holiday cruisers take to the tidal waters, either to join up with the Grand Union Canal at Brentford or the Regent's Canal at Limehouse, not forgetting those intrepid souls who travel down as far as the Medway. So, by way of introduction, we shall look at London's river.

As mentioned before, the journey to the Medway should only be undertaken by the experienced – and, in the case of the tidal Thames, that experience needs to be considerable. Access to the river from the Regent's Canal is via the big ship lock at the end of Limehouse Basin. Those who have only been used to the calm, narrow waters of the canal may find it distinctly alarming to be faced by the rough waters of the Port of London, and the busy traffic of the passenger boats charging up and down the river. It is usually necessary to travel on a rising tide as small boats can make heavy weather of fighting tide and current combined. Those travelling down river will find life easiest if they reach Limehouse at slack water, otherwise the turn into Limehouse Lock can be quite difficult. The operation of the lock is governed by the state of the tide, so it is necessary to check up in advance to find precisely when you can travel.

The trip up river is exhilarating and is quite one of the best ways of seeing the city. All the familiar landmarks are there, starting with Tower Bridge which seems far more impressive from a small boat than it does when seen from land. The first part of the journey takes one past the old warehouses now, sadly, very little used, and then past the City itself, with Wren's spires and the dome of St Paul's still visible, if only just, amid the new office blocks. Modern, graceful Waterloo Bridge leads across to modern, graceless concrete on the south bank. Westminster brings the Houses of Parliament and an easing off of the boat-

Aerial view of the Thames and the Surrey Docks at sunset.

The Thames

trip traffic, so that the scene becomes altogether quieter. There is a pleasant jumble of house-boats at Chelsea and some of the river's most attractive bridges appear, with Albert Bridge perhaps the finest of them all. Kew Bridge offers a mixture of delights, from the monster steam engines of the old pumping station on the north bank to the Royal Botanical Gardens on the south. Ahead is the entrance to the Grand Union at Brentford, where the lock can be used for approximately two hours either side of high tide. At Richmond, the river is crossed by a barrier and the Half Tide Lock. At certain states of the tide, the barrier is lowered and boats can simply pass straight through; at other times they must use the lock. Another three miles of travel and Teddington Lock appears, marking the arrival of the non-tidal river.

The river still has a good deal of its urban character in these early stages. To the south are Kingston, Norbiton and Surbiton, all places which are, no doubt, loved and cherished by their inhabitants, but their lure is unlikely to win against the attractions on the opposite bank. Here one is faced by the splendours of Hampton Court where one can lose oneself, metaphorically speaking, in the past or, in reality, in the maze. The river winds round in a long curve to reach Hampton itself where the famous actor David Garrick made his home, and seeing his house by the river one can only applaud his good sense. After Hampton the river gradually begins to establish more of a rural character and the towns that do turn up seem to present their happiest faces towards the water. Weybridge offers fine surrounding scenery and the entrance to the River Wey (see p. 43). Staines offers huge reservoirs beside the river but not the opportunity to contemplate them in peace, as peace is a rare commodity this close to the roaring jets of Heathrow Airport.

It is a relief to move on to quieter pleasures and the historic meadows of Runnymede. Quite where King John, a much maligned monarch and a far better king than his romanticized brother Richard, signed the Magna Carta is uncertain. Imagination can be allowed to wander to conjure up the scene on that historic day. And a sense of history stays with one as the much photographed and much toured Windsor appears facing the equally famous Eton on the opposite bank. The castle is so magnificent that it

has an air of unreality about it, as if put there as some film mogul's vision of what a royal castle should be like. Eton College, too, has a somewhat theatrical air, but the college chapel is quite simply a beautiful building, one of the greatest, perhaps, of Britain's churches.

Above Windsor the river really comes into its own, flowing through a gentle landscape. There are no dramatic moments here, those will come later, but a pleasant, very English landscape, one to be enjoyed at a leisurely pace. The village of Bray is the first of many delightful small settlements that creep down to the river's edge to dip their toes into the water. A short distance along

are Maidenhead and Boulter's Lock, perhaps the most famous of all the river locks. This was the great gathering place for Victorian and Edwardian boaters who took the Great Western Railway out of London for a day on the river. And one can see why it was so popular, for the lock opens out onto one of the loveliest sections on the Thames, the Cliveden reach. The river is bordered by a high tree-covered hill, and the branches lean over the water to provide a green enclosure to the quiet scene. Those prepared to rise while the rest of the world sleeps and slip out through the morning mists will always remember the experience.

Left above Runnymede meadows.

Left below Boulter's Lock, reputedly the busiest on the Thames.

Above Temple Island, near the start of the Henley Regatta course.

The Thames

Hambleden Mill.

Beyond Cliveden, the river turns again, past Bourne End sitting comfortably on the bend and on to Marlow, a handsome town boasting a fine suspension bridge. A little way beyond is Medmenham and Medmenham Abbey, an infamous spot, home of the Hell Fire Club. This rather pathetic band of Regency bucks squandered time and money on the pretence of being Satanists and very daring. The river winds away from Medmenham until one last bend opens out onto a remarkably straight stretch which every year is home to the Henley Regatta. The town itself, like Marlow, is pleasant and connoisseurs of the hop and barley will be well rewarded if

they stop to sample the locally brewed ale.

Fortified with flagons, the traveller can continue to yet more of those delightful and almost too picturesque villages with which the river abounds – Shiplake and Wargrave facing each other across the water, and Sonning tucked away in a quiet corner. These are delights to be savoured for ahead lies Reading, a town which resolutely refuses to show its best face to the river. The approach is via power station and gasworks followed by the inevitably dull tower blocks. There is, however, the entrance to Kennet & Avon Canal (see p. 146) and the town itself has more to offer than is apparent from the river. In any case, it is all gone soon enough and the delights of Mapledurham lie ahead, delights which

include the last working water-mill on the Thames.

The scenery is now dominated by the wooded hills that surround the river and seem likely to block its path. But the way through appears in the shape of Goring Gap where the river has carved a channel. This is a favourite spot for mooring, with the twin towns of Goring and Streatley joined by a bridge across a complex of foaming weirs. The land now begins to flatten out on the approach to Wallingford, a town which still shows its origins in the surrounding earthworks of the Saxon burgh, and a town which needs to be explored with care if one is to appreciate its special qualities and ancient history. The theme of history can be taken even further back as one

moves towards the Sinodun Hills. They dominate the skyline, two tree-topped mounds, known as Wittenham Clumps, ringed by the ramparts of an Iron Age fort and encampment. And yet more history is to be found in the town of Dorchester, a short way from the river and standing on the Thame not the Thames.

One might begin to complain of a surfeit of history on a Thames journey, for it seems one has hardly left the Sinodun Hills astern before yet another ancient town appears, Abingdon. This is quite definitely a town which offers a splendid river frontage to entice the explorer – rather more so, in fact, than its more famous neighbour upstream, Oxford. As it reaches the city, the river

splits and divides and even acquires the new name of Isis. Oxford is too well known to require any special commendation here, but for those who want to see the best of it from the water, there is no substitute for leaving the motor boat behind and taking a punt up the Cherwell. Here, too, is the start of the Oxford Canal (see p. 131). This is a definite turning point in the character of the river. Below Oxford, in the summer months, the waterway can be almost uncomfortably crowded. Above Oxford it begins to shrink quite noticeably in size and to shrink away, too, from the urban world of cities and towns. It becomes remote, lonely and altogether more peaceful. For 31 miles it keeps itself to itself, with just the occasional

Above A rowing eight passing the ancient town of Abingdon.

lock and riverside pub to interrupt the journey. It is a stretch of river one hesitates to recommend, not because it lacks charm but because so much of its charm comes from its sense of seclusion and peace. Selfishly, perhaps, one wants to keep it to oneself. It is, for many of us, the best of the Thames and the charming town of Lechlade is as good an end to a journey as one could wish. It is hoped one day to extend the navigation for another 11 miles to Cricklade, but when this will happen, or indeed whether it will happen at all, is, for the moment, uncertain. It would, however, be a magnificent addition to an already magnificent river.

The Basingstoke Canal

The Basingstoke is another canal which, after years of neglect, is being restored to navigation, and an exceptionally fine canal it is too. It begins at Woodham on the Wey and originally ran to Basingstoke, 37½ miles with 29 locks. However the Greywell Tunnel has long since collapsed so restoration is planned only as far as Greywell, six miles short of Basingstoke. Even so, restorers are

Below A splendid old steam dredger at work.

Right Wooded sections such as this make the Basingstoke particularly appealing.

faced with a major problem, but one which appears to be well on the way to solution.

The canal was designed from the first as an agricultural rather than an industrial waterway, and its character has changed surprisingly little over the years. Even at Woking, where it passes through the outskirts of the town, it retains a sense of seclusion and is hemmed in by trees. Fourteen locks in two miles then lift it up to open heathland. The locks themselves are found in a splendid wooded setting and end in a spectacularly deep cutting, which gives the surrounding district its name of

Deepcut. The London to Southampton railway line is crossed on an aqueduct, after which the canal opens out into Mytchett Lake and Great Bottom Flash, before one more lock lifts it to the 15-mile-long summit pound. This provides some of the best of the canal scenery, even though it does pass close to the army barracks at Aldershot. The route is peaceful, the canal taking a line as meandering as that of any river through the gentle Hampshire countryside.

Restoration is proceeding rapidly, but already the canal has a lot to offer, if not to the boater then certainly to the towpath walker.

The Wey & Arun Junction Canal

The canal was completed in 1816, and by joining the Wey to the Arun linked the Thames to the south coast. It was a major undertaking with 26 locks in 23 miles and was not a great success. It flourished briefly, and then was closed in 1872. Today, however, work on restoration is well in hand. It is a daunting task since the canal seems almost to have disappeared in places, but enough has been done to show that restoration is at least feasible. At the time of writing, work has reached a point where a lock will soon be opening to allow a boat onto the Wey & Arun for the first time for over a century. It would be a brave soul, though, who would prophesy precisely when the first boat will leave the Wey and pass the length of the canal to join the Arun and the route to the sea.

The Arun

The Arun is navigable from Pulborough to the sea at Littlehampton, but until the completion of the Wey & Arun Canal restoration, it is unlikely to prove of any great interest to inland waterways enthusiasts. It offers 22 miles of cruising waterway, 16 miles of which below Houghton are tidal, but are at present only accessible from the sea. If and when the Wey & Arun is reopened it will make a fine route with many attractions, including a major museum just a short walk from the wharf at Amberley, and Arundel with its castle overlooking the river.

Stopham Bridge, Pulborough.

Below Arundel town and Castle.

The Wey

The Wey runs into the busy Thames, yet remains peaceful and little used. A river which runs through urban south-east England, yet manages to pick its way neatly through the towns to keep a rural character, clearly has a good deal to commend it. The Navigation is not very long, just 19½ miles from Weybridge to Godalming, but it is a route full of interest.

The entrance below Shepperton Lock is neither easy to find nor to negotiate, and once on the river you are faced by the first of 16 locks, and the only one to be manned. Until recently, you could have found yourself sharing the lock with working boats taking grain up to Coxes Mill, but the trade stopped in April 1983. Once beyond that point, the essential nature of the river begins to assert itself as it leaves the town behind and passes between wooded banks. The modern world reappears with the M25, and the old world with the Basingstoke Canal (see p. 40). Then the river is on its own again on a sinuous path increasingly remote from civilization. There is a steady spattering of locks to keep the boater busy, but otherwise there is little to interfere with the quiet enjoyment of the country. The approach to Guildford, however, has rather less charm, but this drab beginning is more than compensated for by a fine passage through the city centre, where a rare example of a treadmill crane can be seen. The route continues on to an equally fine town, Godalming, and here, for the moment at least, it stops.

Below Coxes Mill on the Wey, where boats traded until 1983.

The Grand Union Canal

The Grand Union is, as its name suggests, not one canal but a combination of canals. At its heart is the Grand Junction, built under the direction of William Jessop to provide a through route from London to Birmingham. It was the eighteenth-century equivalent of the M1, a major transport route designed for speed and efficiency with locks built to twice the width of the other Midland canals, so that two narrow boats could sit together snugly, side by side. From the main trunk, a number of conventional narrow canals lead off to serve the main towns along the way. In the 1920s, other canals were scooped up into the organization, notably the Old Union, an earlier exercise in amalgamation, which had joined the Grand Junction to Leicester, and the Regent's Canal in London. Not surprisingly, the different parts of the present Grand Union have very different characteristics, and we shall be looking at the Leicester section later (see p. 138). We shall start our Grand Union tour at the most easterly part of the system, at Limehouse on the Thames.

The entrance from the river has already been described (see p. 34). The basin itself is a wide expanse of water, providing shelter for a fleet of Thames lighters, but once the basin is crossed and the canal itself begins, then the scale changes dramatically. The canal is technically broad with wide locks, but after the river and the Pool of London, it can seem positively Lilliputian. It edges rather tentatively round the outskirts of the city, but nevertheless has the true London flavour. The first section through Bethnal Green comes as something of a surprise, and a pleasant one at that. On the one hand are the busy streets, and on the other the green open spaces of Victoria Park. At Islington there is a glimpse of the old commercial life of the area and the newly fashionable houses before the canal dives into Islington Tunnel to re-emerge to face the Gothic splendours of St Pancras. At Camden Locks, the canalside has been developed with a series of small shops and galleries and the jolly little castellated lock cottage has been restored. The next section, round Regent's Park and London Zoo, is understandably popular with trip boats – and might have been more so had the canal been built as originally planned, straight through the centre of the park. As it is, it skirts round the edge in a deep, tree-lined cutting, crossed by elegant Blow Up Bridge.

Left Regent's Canal in Islington.

Above The aviary at London Zoo.

Below The old machinery beside the Regent's Canal in Camden Town.

The Grand Union Canal

This unusual name was bestowed in 1874 when someone struck a light on a boat loaded with gunpowder. The bridge was pieced together again, but not quite as before. Look closely and you can see grooves cut by tow ropes on the back of the supporting pillars, showing that they were turned round during reconstruction. Soon after leaving the park, the canal passes through the short Maida Hill Tunnel to emerge in Little Venice where, surrounded by appropriate Regency elegance, the Regent's Canal ends.

The Regent's now gives way to the Paddington Arm of the Grand Union. A short arm runs into Paddington Basin itself, a splendid example of how an old warehouse can be rejuvenated to find a new role in the city. The main branch runs off westward for 13 lock-free miles to join the main line. It is not, on the whole, a route much favoured by those in search of picturesque beauty, but it is by no means lacking in interest. Indeed, it even has its picturesque elements, though in a somewhat specialized form. At Kensal Green it skirts the cemetery, one of those great Victorian burial grounds full of imposing, if dour, monuments – very spooky on a foggy morning. To the south is a grandly castellated building where one is not tempted to linger – Wormwood Scrubs. But for those who have ever suffered the miseries of commuter travel, the perfect antidote is on hand. Travel this way in rush hour and you can have the satisfaction of chugging peacefully across the aqueduct over the daily rat race of the North Circular Road. Now, apart from occasional oases of green in such areas as Greenford, the route is very much through industrial west London, much of it very run down, with open spaces marking the disappearance of the old industrial landmarks. Then, at Bull's Bridge, the main line is joined, the line that began at Brentford (see p. 36).

Brentford is an area which still has a busy, commercial life with new, functional warehouses blending well with the equally unfussy canal buildings of the last century. Although the canal is very much within the London area, it has a surprisingly countrified feel to it, which helps to ease the labour of working up Hanwell Locks. At the top is a well-known curiosity, Three Bridges, where the road goes over the canal which goes over the railway. For a while suburbia rules, and names which promise much deliver little: delightful sounding Cowley Peachey turns out to

Above A typical Grand Union bridge, its appeal lies in the graceful simplicity of its lines.

Left above The Gas Works and gasholder with boat at Kensal Green.

Left below A pair of narrow boats about to slide snugly into Hanwell Top Lock.

The Grand Union Canal

be a dredging dump. Here, however, is the start of the Slough Arm giving a five-mile run into Slough, the chief appeal of which is the prospect of a peaceful journey away from other pleasure boats.

At Uxbridge, the nature of the canal scene begins to change. The long run through suburbia is over and rural Grand Union begins. This is the old Grand Junction built to join London to Birmingham by the shortest possible route with little concern for other towns along the way, which are reached only by the various branches. It is not a canal with many dramatic moments, but offers instead a journey through gentle, un-dulating country, where water-mills not tower blocks form the dominant land-marks. Here the route follows the Colne valley, the line marked by attractive watercress beds and somewhat less attractive gravel pits. At Rickmans-worth, however, the pits have been re-claimed and turned into a water-sports complex. The town itself, like so many on this route, scarcely touches the canal, but where it does the waterside is flanked by attractive cottages and stables. Watford, too, is kept at arm's length as the canal deserts the town for the delights of Cassiobury Park. When the canal was built, the landowner insisted that it should be an ornament to his park, and the Company duly obliged with a splen-did, balustraded bridge. Not that much embellishment is needed to make the small hump-backed bridges that dot the Grand Union attractive. They are visual delights, their gentle curves harmonizing with the equally gentle curves of the surrounding land.

The canal passes on, the way marked by a regular procession of locks and an equally regular procession of canalside pubs. There are small, pleasant villages and larger towns, such as Hemel Hempstead. This town has acute schizophrenia, with a charming main

street on one side and a vast complex of roundabouts alongside modern offices on the other. The canal skirts both as it moves out of the Colne valley and into that of the Bourne. Mills continue to feature strongly, and at Bourne End an imaginative conversion of one into a hotel and housing has kept its old character. The hills begin to rise ahead of the canal as it continues to climb to its summit level at Tring. Here Jessop, the engineer, forced his canal through by slicing a great gash through the top of a hill, the Tring cutting. On an undramatic route, this represents one of the few dramatic moments, for the cutting really

is spectacular. It is interesting to note that another engineer, Robert Stephenson, found the same solution to this geographical problem, taking his railway through a parallel cutting.

At the end of the cutting the mood changes again, as the canal plunges down the northern slope of the hills. Near the top of the Marsworth locks is the ornate Bulbourne maintenance yard, where old skills are used in the making of traditional wooden lock gates. The canal sweeps in a wide curve round the Marsworth reservoirs which supply it with water and a rich variety of waterbirds with a home. Here the Wendover Arm

acts as a feeder from the reservoirs, while a little further on the Aylesbury Arm joins the main canal. This is a stretch of water well worth visiting, though it is not for the faint-hearted who baulk at the prospect of 16 locks in six miles. The reward comes in travelling as peaceful and remote a waterway as can be found, though the peace does come to an abrupt end in the centre of Aylesbury.

Continuing northwards, the character of the main line changes very little. There are lovely villages of which Ivinghoe, with its ancient windmill, is among the finest. As the canal reaches the Ouse valley, there is one odd little

Left Marsworth locks and reservoirs at sunrise.

Above Turn-over bridge at Grove Park, Watford.

Below The north end of Blisworth Tunnel.

The Grand Union Canal

Left Stoke Bruerne locks.

Above Part of the Hatton flight of 21 locks.

spot, Church Lock, with church duly present but no visible settlement to provide the congregation. There is a brief urban flirtation with Leighton Buzzard and Linslade, the latter boasting an old pub picturesque enough to tempt the Band of Hope. After that, the canal begins to wander and waver as it follows the river line to the new city of Milton Keynes. The city has taken to the canal, regarding it as something to be cherished rather than ignored, which is good news both for the local citizens and for the canal travellers. Milton Keynes remains, for the time being at least, a brief interlude before another winding section leads away to the railway town of Wolverton and beyond that to the

aqueduct over the Great Ouse. This is a spot with a mixed canal history: an earlier aqueduct collapsed, locks were built down to the river and up again and, finally, the present aqueduct was built to provide airy views across the countryside. Yet another peaceful meander leads up to the Stoke Bruerne locks and the tiny canalside settlement which provides a home to the Waterways Museum. It is much frequented, much photographed and much appreciated by boaters who like to make the most of it, for they are about to dive underground through the 3056-yard-long Blisworth Tunnel.

Beyond Blisworth, the Northampton Arm leads off with a flight of 17 locks ensuring a lively journey towards Northampton and the junction with the Nene (see p. 66). The main line meanwhile continues to wriggle off in the general direction of the M1, which remains mostly out of sight and mercifully out of earshot as well. The canal swings

away to cross an older main road, Watling Street, where the Leicester Arm is met (see p. 138) to be followed by a second long tunnel, Braunston. The village of Braunston itself, at the far end of the tunnel, is very much a canal settlement, built round the junction of the Grand Union and the Oxford Canal, which is briefly joined as a link to the northern section at Napton.

Now the character of the canal changes yet again, as the slow climb up to the Birmingham plateau begins, and the towns along the way make their presence felt far more than on the more southerly sections. The first flight of locks is at Stockton, a mere eight of them, training for what lies ahead. After that exertion, there is a steady spattering of locks, set out in a pleasant, rich agricultural country, before the first of the big towns appears. This is Royal Leamington Spa, though there is not much of the Royal, nor indeed of the Spa, at the canal end of town. It is, however, full of character and well worth a visit if only to gather strength for what lies ahead – the Hatton flight of 21 broad locks. These do not seem too daunting at first, but then you turn a corner into a long straight and they can be seen marching on up the hill in stately procession. Reward comes at the top with a really lovely and peaceful wooded section which leads up to Kingswood Junction. Here a short arm leads across to the Stratford Canal (see p. 118) and the offer of an alternative route into Birmingham. The main line remains lock-free up to Knowle, where the five locks can seem quite tame after the rigours of Hatton.

Solihull marks the real beginning of the Birmingham suburbs, and from here the city begins gradually to close in. Birmingham is Britain's great canal city (see pp. 124-128) and, although it is not just urban but aggressively urban, it offers endless fascination to those who come by water. It is perhaps an acquired taste, but the canal occupies such a private, enclosed world within the great city that those who once become intrigued by it find themselves returning again and again to explore it. This is the industrial world the canal was built to serve, and as you climb up the locks through artificial gorges of factory and warehouse, the long delightful sections of the rural Grand Union at last begin to make sense. To travel the entire route is a pleasure – and a practical lesson in industrial history.

The Lee and Stort

These two connected river navigations offer routes full of contrasts. The upper reaches are as peacefully idyllic as can be imagined, while the lower reaches are urban and bustling with trade.

There are a number of ways of approaching the Lee, the ones most commonly used being via the Limehouse Cut from Limehouse Basin or via the short Hertford Union Canal from the Regent's Canal below Old Ford Lock. But those with a sense of adventure and the necessary experience can enter via the tidal waters of Bow Creek, past the splendid Three Mills conservation area. Only two mills, in fact, remain, but one of these is a rare example of a tide mill, a remarkable building to find in the heart of dockland. From any of these beginnings, the route leads through busy north-east London, through Hackney and Tottenham to Enfield, where the commercial traffic dies away, and the gentler aspects of the river come to

the fore, much enhanced in recent years by the creation of the Lee Valley Regional Park.

The river above Waltham Abbey, which can still boast its old abbey buildings, is particularly pleasing and the steady reclamation of gravel pits and reservoirs has much improved what was a somewhat dull area. By the time Broxbourne is reached, the river is very much devoted to the holiday boater, with chalets instead of factories lining the water. Where industry does appear it does so in style with a number of magnificent maltings and no less splendid water-mills. Just above Broxbourne, the way divides – the Lee continuing towards the north west, the Stort to the north east.

The Lee takes one to the fine old town of Ware, home of the famous great bed. Beyond that is Hertford, a market town which has changed surprisingly little over the years. Between the two is the

start of the New River, the first major water supply scheme in Britain. It was originally built in 1606 by Hugh Myddleton to take fresh water to London, but has been much modernized. Myddleton himself is commemorated in a waterside monument.

The Stort has the same gentle characteristics as the Lee, though it does bump up against Harlow New Town. Again mills and maltings provide the architectural motifs, ranging from the small white weather-boarded mill of Little Hallingbury to the grand maltings with their characteristic pyramidal kilns at Sawbridgeworth. The whole route is quite delightful, largely unspoilt and it offers one of the most attractive cruising routes in the South-East. It all comes to a glorious conclusion at Bishop's Stortford, where navigation ends among the weather-boarded mills, a world away from the narrow streets and tall warehouses of Limehouse.

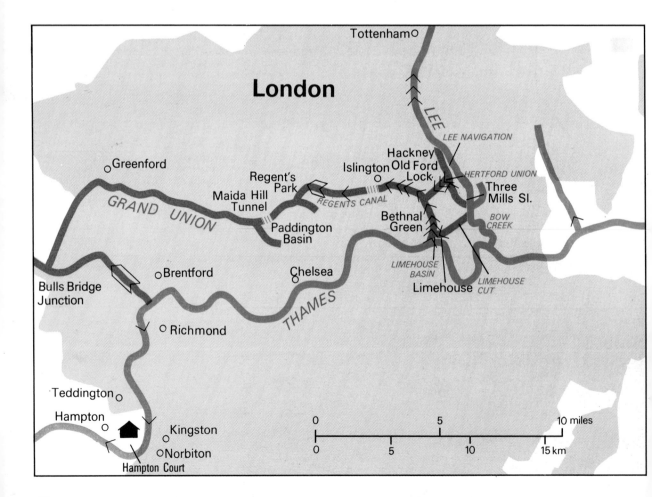

New warehouses at Tottenham on the River Lee.

The Chelmer & Blackwater Navigation

Divorced from other navigable waterways, the Chelmer & Blackwater is mainly used by those who live nearby, or those who come in by sea. It is the sea rather than the surrounding land that gives the route its character, for the land is flat and for much of its length the navigation makes its way peacefully but somewhat dully between muddy banks. But it is a region with the true whiff of salt, for the Blackwater is home to one of the annual barge sailing matches. This is a part of the world with strong associations with barges which sailed in great numbers from the nearby town of Maldon.

The navigation starts among the yachts and dinghies of attractive Heybridge Basin on the tidal Blackwater and then winds its solitary way to Chelmsford. There are no towns along the route, and few landmarks apart from the locks and the tiny medieval church at Ulting.

The Blackwater is home every year to one of the Thames barge sailing matches.

East Anglia

This is an area with a character all its own, a region of big skies and wide horizons. The waterway scene here is quite unlike that of any other part of Britain, for East Anglia remained largely untouched by the canal age. This is not to say that there are no artificial waterways in East Anglia – far from it – but here they were constructed primarily for land drainage, and navigation comes as a bonus. These waterways divide into quite distinct groups. There are two fine rivers, the Nene and the Great Ouse with their tributaries and, in between them, a complex maze of artificial channels known collectively as the Middle Level. Then there is the no less complex system of rivers and lakes, the perennially popular Broads. And there is one other navigable river, rather isolated and not much used by boaters, but perhaps the most famous of them all, the Suffolk Stour.

The Suffolk Stour

The Broads

The Great Ouse

The Cam

The Nene

The Middle Level

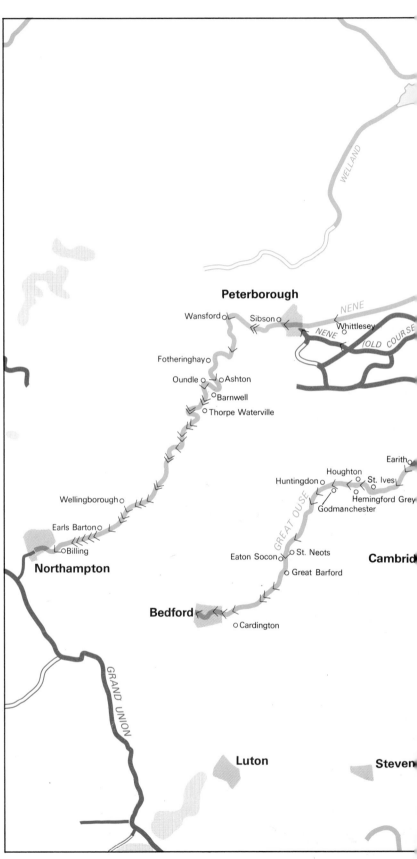

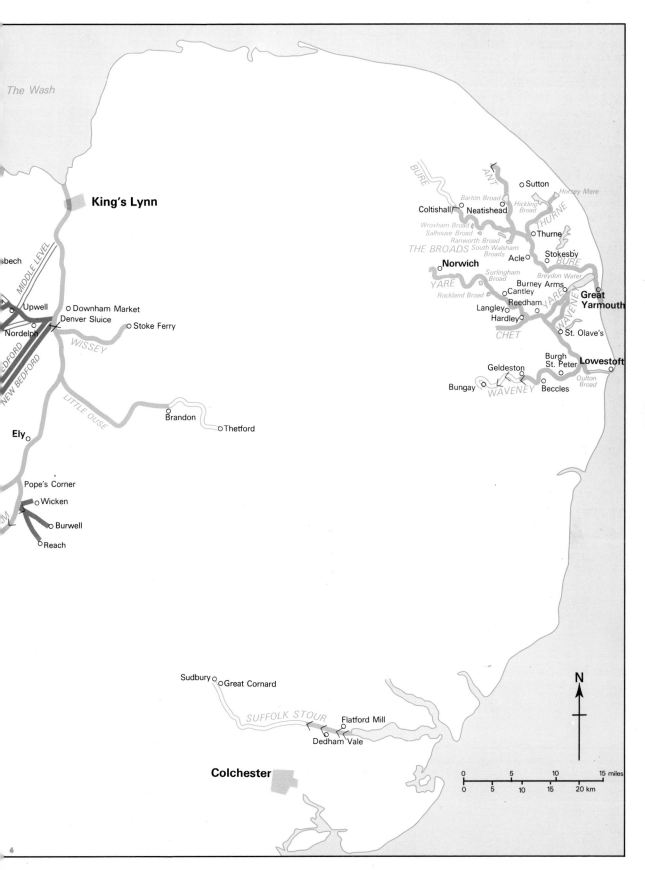

The Wash

King's Lynn

MIDDLE LEVEL

sbech

Upwell
Nordelph
NEW BEDFORD
BEDFORD

Downham Market
Denver Sluice

Stoke Ferry

WISSEY

LITTLE OUSE

Brandon
Thetford

Ely

Pope's Corner

Wicken

Burwell

Reach

Coltishall
Neatishead
Wroxham Broad
Salhouse Broad
Ranworth Broad
THE BROADS

Barton Broad
Hickling Broad

Sutton

Horsey Mere

THURNE

ANT

BURE

Thurne
Stokesby
South Walsham Broads
Acle
BURE

Norwich
Surlingham Broad
Rockland Broad
YARE

Burney Arms
Cantley
Reedham
Langley
Hardley

Breydon Water

Great Yarmouth

YARE

WAVENEY

CHET

St. Olave's

Burgh St. Peter

Geldeston
Bungay
Beccles
WAVENEY

Lowestoft

Oulton Broad

Sudbury
Great Cornard

Flatford Mill
SUFFOLK STOUR
Dedham Vale

Colchester

N

0   5   10   15 miles
0   5   10   15   20 km

The Suffolk Stour

This is a river known to millions who have never stood on its banks, nor perhaps even visited Britain at all. For this is the river which will always be associated with the name of John Constable, and here at Dedham Vale or Flatford Mill you can see the landscape he painted. In some respects it has changed very little, but in one important regard it has changed very much indeed: the river that was first made navigable at the beginning of the eighteenth century is no longer so for much of its length. There is, however, an active restoration group at work and a good deal has already been achieved. At Sudbury, the upper limit of navigation, the old basin at the centre of the town has been restored and very fine it looks too. The river is navigable from here to the first lock at Great Cornard. At the time of writing, plans for restoring this lock have already been drawn up and cash is being raised. On this section one can find the restored Stour lighter, a flat horse-drawn barge which, when seen on the water, seems to bring the world of Constable back to life.

Dedham Vale is currently being restored to its former glory with the towpath being cleared and trees replanted while, at the most famous of all the Stour sites, Flatford Mill, the lock has already been rebuilt, providing access to three miles of river. Although the river is closed at present to power craft until all locks are fully restored, it can be used by craft light enough to be carried round the locks. Those who make the effort will enjoy a beautiful, unspoilt river. There are, indeed, those who argue that the river should be left alone, so that Constable's country can remain at peace, untroubled by the noise of the internal combustion engine.

Above Willy Lott's cottage on the Stour, immortalized by Constable.

Below Flatford Mill, where Constable spent much of his youth, is now used by the Council for the Promotion of Field Studies.

The Broads

This complex area of rivers and shallow lakes is probably the most popular inland boating area in Britain, with only the Thames offering serious competition. And, as with the Thames, pleasure boating on the Broads has a history going back over a hundred years. The nature of the holiday trade has, however, changed greatly in recent times, for now the motor cruiser has largely taken over from the sailing boat. Checking through the brochures of two of the largest hire companies produced the following remarkable figures: they were offering 59 sailing craft for hire and nearly 800 motor cruisers. Such figures show both the decline in popularity of traditional Broads sailing and the huge growth of motor cruising which can make these waters in midsummer as busy as a main road. Inevitably, there has been controversy over the relative merits of sail and power. The proponents of sail complain about the noise of the cruisers, the pollution (unproven) and the erosion caused by speeding power boats (all too plain). The opposition points to the growth of motor cruisers as a means of opening up the Broads to thousands who have no wish to learn the mysteries of reefing and tacking. And they claim, with some justification, that there is an élitist element among the sailors who wish to keep the Broads exclusive. As readers are entitled to some indication of where an author stands, I shall say no more than that I have always enjoyed my time on the Broads – and have yet to step on board a vessel fitted with a motor. That said, it is up to the individual to decide which is the best way to travel and not to let the prejudices of others – including authors – deter them.

The Broads can be roughly divided into two systems. To the north is the complex based on the rivers Bure, Thurne and Ant; to the south that of the Yare and Waveney. Both systems have a common start at Great Yarmouth, where the tidal Yare leads off to a tidal lake, Breydon Water. Great Yarmouth itself is unashamedly brash, a seaside resort still set in the world of McGill postcards. The river here is quite tricky, being tidal, as is Breydon Water, though at least the channel is clearly marked.

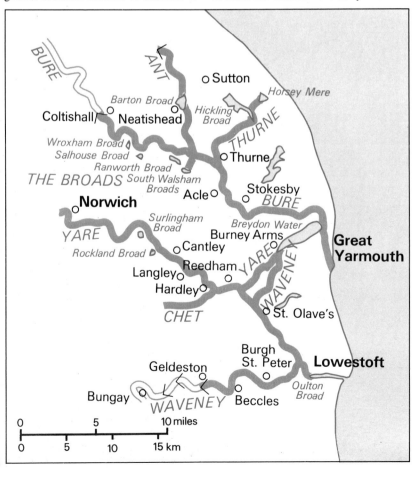

The Broads

Stray from that channel and you will find yourself called upon to practise the ancient Broadland art of quanting, or pushing off with a pole. In unpowered craft, quanting is the way you move on windless days; in powered craft it is usually reserved for groundings. At the end of Breydon Water, the Bure leads off to the north, while at the southern end the route divides between the Yare and the Waveney.

The Yare itself is a fascinating river which still carries commercial traffic – vessels trading to Norwich. Pleasure boaters are liable to find themselves sharing the water with small coasters – small that is in terms of coastal shipping, but seeming huge in relation to one's own small cruiser. At Berney Arms one reaches the first and the grandest of the many windmills that characterize the Broads. It is seven storeys high and, like many of the others, was used to power drainage pumps, for much of the land here was only reclaimed with a good deal of effort. Here, too, is a safe mooring, clear of the swirling currents of

the tidal river, providing an opportunity to pause and admire the windmill – or the pub next door. The river has all the characteristics that one associates with this part of the world. It is gentle and wide, flowing between high banks of reeds. Some consider this a featureless and drab landscape, but others have come to love it for its own special qualities, for the dry rattle of wind-bent reeds, the majestic march of clouds across a vast sky and for the sight and sounds of the rich variety of waterfowl. These are the pleasures which the Yare and the other Broadland rivers offer in full measure.

At Reedham, a straight artificial channel – the New Cut – leads south into the Waveney, while just beyond is the entrance to the tortuous River Chet. It offers a pleasant excursion to the little market town of Loddon. Here, too, is an obelisk that marks a river boundary, dividing off that part of the Yare which is the responsibility of Yarmouth from that which belongs to Norwich. Short dykes lead off the river at Hardley and Langley

Above Sailing boats on Horsey Mere.

Right The head of navigation on the Waveney at Norwich.

The Broads

offering quiet moorings out of the main stream. At Cantley, the scene is dominated by the sugar beet processing factory. Four miles beyond that is Short Dyke which leads to the largest of the Yare Broads, Rockland, where there are moorings and a pub. Beyond the turn, the character of the main river begins to change, as woodland takes the place of the familiar reeds along the banks, and a little shady cutting leads off to Surlingham Broad. This area is under the care of the Norfolk Naturalist Trust.

As the river nears Norwich it seems to lose still more of its original character, and the steep slopes that surround it give the lie to the notion that Norfolk is flat. Norwich itself provides more than enough justification for making the trip, for if not the largest of county towns it is certainly one of the loveliest, rivalling York and Lincoln. It has a splendid cathedral, a profusion of old buildings and the river has always been of vital

importance to the city, as witnessed by the tenth-century Water Gate. It is a memorable end to the voyage.

Retracing one's steps back to Breydon Water brings one to the start of the Waveney, which forms the boundary between Norfolk and Suffolk. The first section of the river follows a winding course between reed beds and mud banks, a lonely river that scarcely touches town or village. A rare exception is St Olave's, a single street of old houses running down to the river. Beyond that is more marshland until Oulton Dyke is reached, leading off to Oulton Broad and Lowestoft. This is one of the most popular, and busiest, stretches of water in the whole district. Here you are likely to meet anything from a flotilla of sailing dinghies to a power boat race – and, as the base for the largest hire fleet in Britain, you will certainly meet plenty of cruisers. From here there is access to the old fishing port of Lowestoft whose

fleets, unlike the hire boats of the Broads, are sadly depleted from the great days when the trawlers and drifters set out in their hundreds to pursue the herring.

The river meanwhile meanders off to more peaceful regions, past Burgh St Peter, with its unusual thatched church, to Beccles, a town still clad in the quiet dignity of the eighteenth century. The last few miles to Geldeston are pure delight, a peaceful meander through meadows and banks lined with willows. Originally it was possible to go on to Bungay, and light craft can be taken round the derelict lock on a special ramp.

The northern system centres on the longest of the rivers, the Bure. It begins as a fast-flowing tidal river which, like so many rivers in their lower reaches, makes its way through mud banks, the ruins of windmills providing the few points of interest. At Stokesby it calms

Left Commercial traffic can still be seen on the River Yare.

Above Ranworth Broad.

Below Windmill, yacht and cruiser – a typical Broads mixture at Thurne.

The Broads

down sufficiently for safe mooring. Here, too, the mud retreats and the river scenery improves with a border of waving reeds. Beyond that is Acle and Acle Bridge, a popular stopping place. There is a pub crowned by a weather vane in the form of a trading wherry. The scenery continues to be pleasing and peaceful up to the entrance to the Thurne, and there are some interesting little spots, such as the ruined St Benet's Abbey which has a windmill built into its walls. The river now takes a line through an artificial cutting, but the old line can still be followed to peaceful South Walsham Broad. Just beyond the cutting is a major river crossroads, the junction with the Ant, followed by the entrance to Ranworth Broad, which is closed to powered craft. The river now becomes ever more convoluted as it twists off towards one of the lakes which can be visited, Salhouse Broad. The next in the series is very popular, for Wroxham Broad rivals Oulton for the dubious privilege of being the busiest stretch of water in the district. It is,

nevertheless, a splendid place, especially popular with sailing enthusiasts. Those who do not wish to mingle with the crowds can continue on to the lovely little village of Coltishall where navigation ends.

The two rivers passed along the way offer their own varied delights; the Thurne in particular has what might be termed a special attraction: turning into the river from the Bure, Thurne Dyke appears. This is a spot blessed both by a well preserved windmill and, when she's not out under sail, the last surviving example of the vessels that once traded throughout the region, the wherry *Albion*. And, as a last extra attraction, there is a pleasant pub at the end of the dyke. The river moves on to the broad Womack Water and Potter Heigham of the famous – or infamous – bridge. The arches are both low and narrow, and large cruisers are taken through by a pilot at full speed, not a course recommended to the inexperienced, and even the experienced blanch at the prospect. The river then goes on to a complex of

The notorious tight squeeze through the bridge at Potter Heigham.

lakes, including the vast, but shallow, Hickling Broad and through a narrow, tree-lined channel to Horsey Mere, and another splendid and well preserved wind pump.

If the Thurne is secluded, then the Ant is even more so, a narrow and often tortuous channel that winds on to Barton and Sutton Broads. Here one can see evidence of reed cutting for thatch, and might meet one of the heavily-laden reed barges. Essentially, it is a part of the Broads for those who want to get away from the crowds, and if one were to choose anywhere in the whole system to spend a peaceful night in tree-shaded seclusion, then it would be at Neatishead off Barton Broad. Such seclusion is increasingly difficult to find in a Broadland summer, but this is a unique region and it still offers the full range of experience from the bustle of the popular resorts to complete tranquillity and peace.

The Great Ouse

The bridge chapel at St Ives.

This river first becomes navigable at Bedford and remains navigable all the way to the Wash. That boats can make this journey at all is due to the joint efforts of the Anglian Water Authority and the Great Ouse Restoration Society. New locks and weirs were built after the old had fallen into disuse and ruin, and in 1978 the entire waterway was restored to its former glory. All lovers of Britain's waterways should throw their hats in the air and give three hearty cheers, for the river offers a wonderfully rich mixture of remote rural sections and fine old towns.

Bedford is not perhaps a town that would feature on anyone's list of the most beautiful in Britain. It is an unpretentious, workaday sort of town, but the river sees some of the best of it and, once clear of the suburbs, runs out into a lovely, isolated valley, punctuated only by the new locks. These are a mixture of the conventional and the unconventional, for there are two types of gate – the familiar mitre gates, and guillotines which are raised and lowered vertically, but without the fatal consequences that

the name might suggest. The second lock bears a name famous in transport history, Cardington. The nearby airfield was the great centre for airship construction and flying, and the huge hangar which housed the unhappy R101 still stands. The place is almost equally famous as the home of the Whitbread family, several members of which are depicted in marble in the village church, their sobriety being more in keeping with their present surroundings than with their past occupation. None of this, however, impinges very closely on the waterway which continues to follow its own quiet path.

The villages that do touch the river tend to be peaceful, out-of-the-way spots such as Great Barford and Eaton Socon, villages that still belong to the natives and have not been put on the tourist map. Even the first town of any size, St Neots, is a quiet unassuming sort of place, chiefly remarkable for its church, an unusually grand building, mostly dating from the fifteenth century with a 120-feet-high tower. The bridge,

however, is modern and somewhat dull, which certainly could not be said of the next river crossing. The bridge joining Godmanchester to Huntingdon has stood there for six centuries, which makes it quite modern in these surroundings. Godmanchester was a Roman fort and Huntingdon, a Saxon settlement, boasts a twelfth-century hospital and a sixteenth-century grammar school, which numbers Oliver Cromwell among its old boys. The river is by no means overpowered by all this antiquity, for it has its own charms, including a delightful Chinese-style footbridge. And, leaving the towns behind, it offers some fine scenery. The old water-mill at Houghton is followed almost at once by Hemingford Grey, with its magnificent church standing right at the water's edge. Two miles further on and this impressive catalogue of antiquities is completed at St Ives, where the river is crossed by one of Britain's finest

The Great Ouse

old bridges. The six stone arches are crowned by a tiny chapel where travellers could pause to offer up a prayer for a safe journey.

Beyond St Ives, the river increasingly takes on the character of the Fens and even briefly, and somewhat surprisingly, becomes tidal at Earith. This is due to the arrival of the artificial cutting of the New Bedford River, which runs straight and true into the Wash. Those anxious to reach the Wash in the shortest possible time should follow this route which has, in truth, little but its straightness to commend it. Those with time to spare can continue on the far pleasanter, if more circuitous old river route. This passes through reedy banks and strangely empty, almost desolate land, though there is a treat ahead for steam engine enthusiasts. Stretham Old Engine was installed in 1831 for land drainage. It no longer works but has been preserved together with the scoop wheel that lifted water from Stretham Mere and deposited it in the river. The site is open to visitors.

The waterway broadens as it is joined first by the Cam then by the Soham Lode, navigable by small craft. Ahead is the quintessential Fenland city of Ely, once isolated on an island before drainage work surrounded it by dry land. The city announces itself well in advance by its cathedral graced with tower and octagonal lantern, the latter being best described as a Gothic dome. Nothing quite like it can be found anywhere else. At a more earthly level, the city has a fine range of riverside maltings.

Beyond Ely, the river is joined by a number of navigable tributaries, starting with the Lark which can be used by larger craft as far as Judes Ferry, 13 miles up river. This is followed by the Little Ouse, which was once navigable as far as Thetford, but today navigation stops at Brandon Staunch, 13 miles upstream. It offers a pleasant diversion from the main river, as does the Wissey which is navigable for ten miles to Stoke Ferry. Then one reaches Denver Sluice, which either lifts you up to the tidal river at high tide or drops you down to it at low tide. Immediately beyond that is the far end of the New Bedford River. The remainder of the journey is frankly unattractive, and the fast, difficult current does little to encourage pauses even at such attractive spots as Downham Market. The final 16 miles of tideway can only really be recommended to those who really need to reach King's Lynn and the Wash.

The Cam

Navigable for 14½ miles as far as Cambridge, the Cam offers a splendid contrast between the absolute wilderness of the Fens and the sophisticated urbanity of the university town. At the start of the journey at Pope's Corner the wildness has it, especially on a windy day when, apart from the comforts offered by the Fish and Duck Inn, this part of the world can seem unbelievably bleak and isolated. Burwell Lode and Upware Lock mark the arrival of a complex waterways junction. One can run straight on to Burwell with its splendid church, take another branch to Reach or a third to Wicken. There is perhaps no better place than Wicken Fen to capture the true atmosphere of this region, for it is the last of the fens of the Great Level to remain undrained. Once it covered 2500 square miles, now this one square mile is all that remains, preserved by the National Trust. It is a naturalist's paradise, with 300 different flowering plants, an astonishing 5000 species of insect, and numerous birds which can be watched from the hide. The small windmill with its scoop wheel was built in 1905 and originally stood on Adventurers' Fen.

Bottisham Lock with its guillotine gate marks the start of the busier section of the river as it nears Cambridge. The river is navigable through the town along the famous Backs where the college lawns reach down to the water. Here one can visit one of the most famous of riverside scenes, King's College Chapel. There can be few finer ends to any river journey.

Left above Ely Cathedral.

Left below The 'Chinese' wooden footbridge built in 1827, Godmanchester.

Right Wicken Fen.

The Nene

The Nene is an ideal river for those in search of peaceful cruising and quiet pleasures. It is uncrowded, meandering and altogether delightful. But those who wish to savour such delights must pay a price – hard work. There are 38 locks on the Nene, all built with mitre gates at the top and guillotine gates at the bottom, and it is the latter in all but one case that provide the healthy exercise. To raise them requires something like 100 turns of the handle and at Ditchford, Rush Mills and Northampton, where the gates are curved, about 150 turns are required. And, to add to the labour, the gates are normally kept open, so all users have a double load of windings. Travel the Nene from end to end and you will have turned that handle 8000 times! Those who do rarely seem to mind, for the river amply repays the effort.

Navigation begins at Northampton, where there is a junction with an arm of the Grand Union (see p. 51). It is an attractive start, for the town makes much of its river and the first lock is set in Beckett Park. Northampton has been much beset by road improvements in recent years, but none of this impinges greatly on the river and the suburbs are soon cleared. The first dozen miles to Wellingborough are punctuated at regular intervals by a lock a mile, so there is ample time to enjoy the country-side. Northamptonshire is a much underrated county and it is a pleasure to find that its villages, built of rich, warm ironstone are largely unspoilt. It is rather like finding the Cotswolds with no crowds. The one exception occurs at Billing, where a number of lakes have been joined together to create the Billing Aquadrome, a jolly spot in the summer, a bit like an inland Clacton. Those in search of quieter pleasures can cruise on to Earls Barton, with the finest Saxon church tower in Britain. Not that it is necessary to leave the river at all to find pleasure, for it is a gentle stream that slips its way between the lush water meadows.

At Wellingborough the steady progression of locks continues, but with mercifully widening gaps between them. Not that the crew can relax altogether, for there are a number of splendid old bridges that require a good deal of care if they are to be safely negotiated. Higham Bridge is the lowest, but the best is Islip Bridge with its nine stone arches. All the small villages and towns along the way are worth exploring, as the river continues to twist and turn through the peaceful land. One could single out Thorpe Waterville for its quite magnificent medieval thatched barn, and among the purely river pleasures pick Lilford Lock, set among trees with a

little bridge and lock cottage of local stone.

At Barnwell, the old mill has been converted into a restaurant, offering a chance to stoke up the personal boilers after all that lock work. Then the river goes into one of its more extravagant convolutions to take it round Oundle, providing views of the town from every conceivable angle, views always dominated by the tall spire of the church. On the opposite bank stands Ashton, which as well as being yet another of those fine stone villages is also home to the National Conker Championships. As the river continues its serpentine course, another church appears on the horizon

to dominate the view. Fotheringhay church is arguably the finest of all the Nene churches, with its great lantern tower topped by a golden falcon, emblem of the House of York. Royal associations are strong in Fotheringhay, for Richard III was born here, and the thistles that grow on the castle mound are said to have sprung from seeds scattered by Mary Queen of Scots shortly before she was beheaded in 1587.

The river executes another of its about turns at Wansford-in-England, a curious name that has its origins in one of Nene's odder stories. The local drunk is said to have gone to sleep on a haycock and snored his way through the rising of

Left The peaceful windings of the Nene.

Above The ancient bridge and church at Fotheringhay.

The Nene

the river's flood waters, which can indeed rise remarkably quickly. Drunk and haycock floated away and the unfortunate man woke to find himself he knew not where. Supplied with the name Wansford which meant nothing to him, he demanded more precise details. 'Wansford in England' came the reply, and Wansford-in-England it remains. Had the drunk stayed on his haycock he would have been carried on through lovely wooded reaches to Peterborough.

At Sibson, on the outskirts of the city, is the Nene Valley Railway, a steam line offering a five-and-a-half-mile journey on summer weekends. This is one of the most popular preserved railways and one with a distinctly exotic character, for locomotives and carriages come from all over Europe. Non steam enthusiasts can continue into Peterborough, where they will find that every effort has been made to provide for boaters, with first-class moorings and facilities. The city is a mixture of the old and the new, with the old cathedral still dominating the skyline. Peterborough also marks the end of the hard work, as the 37th lock is the last one that has to be operated manually. For many this will also mean journey's end; another five miles leads to the electrically operated, and oddly named, Dog-in-a-Doublet Lock, which gives access to the tidal river.

The tideway suffers all the disadvantages that one might expect on these east coast rivers, running rapidly between high mud banks which obliterate the view. Once it reached the sea at a point four miles below Wisbech, but changes in the river pushed Wisbech away from the sea, so that there is now a 12-mile run to open water. This proved the end of the town as a thriving port so that, in effect, the clock was stopped. The river front remains as it was 200 years ago, a handsome Georgian port.

The last few miles should be left to experienced boaters in seaworthy craft. Tides and currents are fierce, but this, the loneliest stretch of the river with its wildfowl and the tang of the seas, has its own appeal.

Left A typical guillotine lock on the Nene.

Right Salter's Lode Lock, the start of the Middle Level.

The Middle Level

Those who really want to get away from it could do far worse than set off along the Middle Level, a complex of navigable drainage channels joining the Nene to the Great Ouse. There are two principal through routes: the first from Stanground Sluice near Peterborough via Whittlesey and the old River Nene to Well Creek and the Great Ouse; the second route is via the Old Bedford River. There are other navigable channels to tempt the truly adventurous.

There are few towns and villages along the Middle Level which can seem a strange and lonely place. Stanground Sluice drops boats down from the Nene into the King's Dyke which leads off towards Whittlesey, a pleasant little town with a pub oddly named the Letter B, which once had companions A, C and D. Here too is a lock and the infamous Whittlesey bend, the sharpest to be found on any British waterway. It can be successfully negotiated by boats up to 46 feet long, provided it is taken slowly

and cautiously. Soon the first of many aquatic crossroads is reached with the option of going south, to be faced by the very low Exhibition Bridge, north up to the Twenty Foot Drain, straight and rather dull, or to take the most pleasant route which wanders off towards March and the old line of the Nene. A second crossing soon appears, by which time you will have appreciated why all those who travel this way need good maps.

March comes as something of a surprise, a railway town in the middle of the Fens, but it is soon only a memory as the Middle Level returns to its lonely paths. Marmount Priory Lock provides access to Well Creek, which has very much the air of the Dutch canals about it – not too surprising, perhaps, given the role of Dutch engineers such as Cornelius Vermuyden in creating the system. The illusion is complete with the arrival of Upwell and Outwell, villages facing each other across the waterway, very much in the Dutch manner. A short aqueduct

carries the channel across the Middle Level Main Drain. There is one more pretty little village, Nordelph, before Denver Sluice and the Great Ouse.

The main alternative to this route is to turn south on the Old Nene at Flood's Ferry, and on to the Forty Foot Drain. The landscape is wide and open, and the reclaimed land rich. It is not to everyone's taste, but no one can deny its unique character. The Forty Foot leads to the Old Bedford River, which runs straight as a Roman road, with the New Bedford alongside to keep it company. It is not, one has to say, unduly exciting. It eventually arrives at Well Creek, close by the junction with the Great Ouse.

The Middle Level can perhaps best be described as an acquired taste, but those who have acquired it will tell you that the mixture of intricate waterways and open skies has a real fascination.

Below Well Creek.

The North-East

This is an area dominated by big, wide rivers which sweep through a mainly flat landscape. It may not sound like the recipe for an exciting holiday, but there is one other ingredient in this north-eastern mixture which makes all the difference: this is a region where modernization has opened up the waterways to heavy commercial traffic. Holiday makers will find themselves sharing the water with a variety of craft, from big motor barges to small coasters. There are quiet and peaceful waterways in the area as well, as attractive as any in the country. There is certainly no other region which can offer a wider range of waterway experiences.

The Welland

The Witham and Fossdyke

The Trent

The Sheffield & South Yorkshire Navigation

The Aire & Calder Navigation

The Ouse (Yorkshire)

The Ure and Ripon Canal

The Wharfe

The Derwent

The Ancholme

The Hull and the Driffield Navigation

The Chesterfield Canal

The Idle

Ripon
Swale Nab
Boroughbridge
Malton
Driffield
RIPON
URE
Harrogate
Nun Monkton
York
DRIFFIELD
Stamford Bridge
DERWENT
Pocklington
POCKLINGTON
WHARFE
OUSE
Tadcaster
Beverley
HULL
Hull
Bradford
Leeds
Cawood
East Cottingwith
Selby
SELBY
Castleford
Goole
Ferrybridge
Great Heck
Stanley
AIRE
Knottingley
Trent Falls
South Ferriby
Huddersfield
CALDER
DON
Thorne
Keadby
Scunthorpe
Barnsley
STAINFORTH & KEADBY
East Butterwick
West Butterwick
Brigg
Grimsby
Doncaster
SHEFFIELD & SOUTH YORKSHIRE
Sprotbrough
West Stockwith
Owston Ferry
Conisbrough
Misterton
East Stockwith
ANCHOLME
Sheffield
Rotherham
Bawtry
IDLE
Gringley
Gainsborough
Scofton
Retford
CHESTERFIELD
Worksop
Torksey Junction
FOSSDYKE
Lincoln
Chesterfield
Dunham
Saxilby
High Marnham
Bardney
Mansfield
WITHAM
Chapel Hill
Newark
Farndon
TRENT
Derby
Nottingham
Holme Pierrepont
Boston
Nottingham
SOAR
Spalding
WELLAND
King's Lynn
TRENT & MERSEY
Deeping St. James
Leicester
Stamford
Crowland
ASHBY
COVENTRY
OXFORD
Birmingham
NENE
NEW BEDFORD
GREAT
OUSE
Coventry
GRAND UNION
Northampton

0   5   10   15 miles
0   5   10   15   20 km

N

The Welland

The river is only navigable for 24½ miles, nine miles of which are tidal. Once it was a river of considerable importance, navigable as far as Stamford and with a thriving boat-building industry at Spalding. Today the commercial trade has gone and the navigation has shrunk, but what remains is of considerable interest.

The head of navigation is the derelict lock at Deeping St James. The countryside is the flattest of flat Fenland, but nearby is a reminder that land drainage and reclamation is nothing new in this part of the world. This is part of the Car Dyke built by the Romans and, some say, used for navigation as well as drainage, though there is little evidence to support that claim. The first town to be met is Crowland which, although a mile from the river, is well worth a visit if only to see the unique medieval Trinity Bridge. The bridge is triangular in plan, built to cross three streams which have since dried up.

The river is seen at its best in spring, for as it approaches Spalding it passes through acre upon acre of bulb fields, so that the feeling that you have strayed onto a Dutch waterway is very strong, an illusion scarcely dispelled at Spalding where many fine houses line the river bank. A mile downstream, Fulney Lock gives access to the tideway and the Wash.

Below Spalding, an important agricultural town, is renowned above all for its fields of tulips and hyacinths.

Right Trinity Bridge, Crowland, built in the thirteenth century

The Witham and Fossdyke

The Witham is yet another of those rivers which empty into the Wash and, as with the others, the tideway tends to be featureless, muddy and suitable only for seagoing craft. It is possible to leave the tideway for the navigable drains, but these are straight and dull. The river would seem to have little to recommend it were it not for the towns met with along the way, starting with Boston. This is a fascinating spot with rich historical associations, not least with its namesake across the Atlantic. For this Boston, too, was in its day a great port and it was from here that the *Mayflower* set sail in 1620. There are still many reminders of the past in the old warehouses that line the quay and the rather grand Customs House of 1725. There are reminders, too, that land drainage has played an important part in the region with the five-sailed Maud Foster windmill. When the land was drained it was grazed by sheep, and the wool trade has its own memorial in the sixteenth-century guildhall. It was a prosperous town displaying its prosperity to the world in the Boston Stump, a church tower that stands more than 270 feet above the river.

The river above Boston is less than exciting with few settlements and scarcely even a bridge to mark progress. There is a flurry of interest around Dogdyke, with the village of Chapel Hill, a ferry boat inn, the entrance to the

The twelfth-century Glory Hole, properly known as High Bridge, in Lincoln.

The Witham and Fossdyke

disused Sleaford Navigation and nearby Tattershall Castle. The latter, which is open to the public, is a good example of a fortified house. Elsewhere, the villages keep their distance from the water. Bardney comes nearest to making actual contact but, as with the other small settlements, it is a pleasant but undemonstrative sort of place. Indeed, the main interest on this reach is the distant view of the towers of Lincoln Cathedral.

The first glimpse of the city is less than enthralling, as the river passes through one of those modern industrial estates where the buildings give no hint of what goes on inside. Disappointment, however, is short lived, for the city centre is magnificent. You pass through the famous Glory Hole, more properly known as High Bridge, a twelfth-century bridge carrying the High Street, which has a timber-framed sixteenth-century house, over the water. It is rather like a miniature version of the old London Bridge. The city itself is dominated by the cathedral, but the river provides memories of its old commercial life. Navigation ends at Brayford Pool, surrounded by docks and warehouses that date from the days when Lincoln was indeed a busy port. At the opposite end of the pool is the entrance to the Fossdyke Canal, built by the Romans to join Lincoln, their settlement of Lindum Colonia, to the Trent. There is a very special feeling in taking a boat across the pool to traverse 1800 years of history. Lincoln is notable as a city that bears the marks of history at every turn, but nowhere is this more true than here on the water.

The canal itself is just over 11 miles long, with just one lock, and shows the Roman fondness for straight lines. Being largely confined between high banks, it offers little chance of seeing anything at all. Halfway down is Saxilby which turns a pleasant face to the canal and at the end is Torksey where the canal runs into the tidal Trent.

Below Saxilby.

The Trent

This great river is navigable for 93 miles from its confluence with the Humber at Trent Falls to the junction with the Trent & Mersey Canal at Derwent Mouth. It plays a vital role in inland navigation, linking together the waterways of the North-East with those of the Midlands.

The river divides into two distinct sections: the long tideway that stretches from the Humber to Cromwell Lock, a distance of 52½ miles; and the upper reaches. Unlike many river navigations, the tidal Trent carries a not inconsiderable pleasure boat traffic between the North and the Midlands. It is like the others, however, in that it is a river which requires skill and experience if it is to be navigated safely, for in addition to problems with tides and currents there are seagoing ships using the water.

The northern end at Trent Falls has more the character of a wide estuary than of an inland river. Vessels come in from the North Sea or from the port of Goole and swing round into the wide expanses of the Trent. This waterway once carried a considerable canal boat traffic, but only the very experienced should attempt the passage, and many hire companies will not permit hirers to take their boats along this route. A much easier route is available for boats from the North-East via the Stainforth & Keadby Canal (see p. 78) which joins the river at Keadby, nine miles from the river mouth. The first essential for any-one travelling this route is to know the state of the tides. Boats turning south out of Keadby Lock still have more than 40 miles to travel before Cromwell Lock and the end of the tideway. There are a number of places along the way, however, where boats can turn out of the river to find safe moorings, but those wishing to make the whole tideway trip in one go have to get their timing right. Canal boats pushing upstream against the current have enough to contend with as it is, without the problems of fighting the tide as well. The ideal is to leave

Below A peaceful evening on the Trent.

The Trent

Keadby at slack water and use the rising tide to help the passage. Coming in the opposite direction is more complex, as it is all too easy to be swept past the lock entrance by the combined forces of current and tide. Again, arrival at slack water is best, and the easiest way to approach the lock is to go slightly beyond and then turn and approach against the current. It is, however, essential to check lock opening hours in advance. There is one further point for those planning this journey along the long tideway: take an anchor and an adequate length of anchor chain. This is advisable for all tidal rivers, but is absolutely essential on the Trent.

Keadby is a small but busy port on the west bank of the Trent, facing across the water towards Scunthorpe where the steel works light the evening sky. Once out on the river, boats pass under two bridges, one rail, one road, the last to be met with before Gainsborough. There is little to see apart from the high flood banks, but there is no shortage of interest on a river busy with coasters and barges. The villages of East and West Butterwick peer shyly at each other over the banks, Owston Ferry puts in a brief appearance, then East and West Stockwith arrive with the first chance to pull off the river.

At West Stockwith, the River Idle appears, the junction marked by an attractive mill building with an old steam engine house (see p. 88). Then comes West Stockwith Basin with excellent moorings protected behind a lock and access to the Chesterfield Canal (see p. 88). Those continuing straight on will find little change in the scenery until Gainsborough, a town which has all the appearance of a small sea port with extensive wharves and warehouses. This marks a definite staging post in the river, for beyond this point the commercial traffic dwindles and the river itself becomes noticeably more tortuous. The giant mill and silo at Gainsborough remain the most prominent landmark for many miles, seeming to appear at every point of the compass as the boat changes direction.

Villages appear intermittently, all but hidden by the high banks until Torksey is reached and the entrance to the Fossdyke (see p. 74). At Dunham is one of the rare bridges; river travellers have the advantage over those on the road who have to pay tolls for the privilege of using it. Here, too, the dead flatness which characterizes the landscape to this point

begins to give way to a steady undulation of hill and hollow while, at High Marnham, the first of the Trent power stations appears, with a cluster of cooling towers. No river in Britain can boast so many power stations and it is interesting to note how often the provision of power has been accompanied by handsome buildings, windmills and water-mills in the past and the elegant curving cooling towers of our own age. Another nine miles of bends brings Cromwell Lock, the end of the tideway and the start of calmer waters.

Beyond the lock there is a marked change in the scenery. Villages no longer lurk behind the banks but show their faces to the river and soon the loveliest

Above One of the massive weirs on the Trent.

Right Newark Castle, built in 1125, was ruined during the Civil War.

of the Trent towns appears – Newark. This is a town with a rich mixture of ingredients, all of which have their effect on the river scene. It is approached through an artificial cutting, bordered by maltings and a brewery. Then the bridge appears and the castle, which can seem little more than a heap of rubble viewed

from the town side, offers a very handsome façade to the river. Beyond that is the lock, bordered by old warehouses and town houses that seem to tumble down the slope towards the water. Up in the town centre is the Georgian market square and the vast parish church, lording it over them all.

Beyond Newark the river scenery becomes more attractive, and the same could be said of the riverside villages, starting with Farndon. The Trent is a river with remarkably few bridges, and a large number of ferry boat inns. These, together with the ubiquitous power stations (at Trent Port you can stand at the end of the jetty and actually see three of them), give the river much of its personality. The rest comes from the increasingly convoluted course, punctuated by locks with massive weirs alongside. This theme remains up to Holme Pierrepont where old gravel workings have been converted into an international rowing course, and where the Nottingham suburbs creep up towards the river. The centre of Nottingham is marked by the ornate iron bridge which gives the Trent Bridge cricket ground its name. The route now continues by an artificial cut, the Nottingham Canal.

The canal itself tends to creep somewhat surreptitiously through the city, skirting the high Castle rock, alongside which is one of the pubs that claims the title of oldest in Britain, the Trip to Jerusalem. Here, too, is a wharf which was once home to the most famous of all canal carrying companies, Fellows, Morton & Clayton, and is now home to a canal museum. Emerging from the far side of the city, the canal rejoins the river close by a waterway junction with the River Soar leading south (see p. 138), the Erewash leading north (see p. 140) and the Trent going straight on past a pleasing jumble of holiday chalets. A large weir, to be treated with caution, sits just below the M1 bridge, then there is a short journey to Derwent Mouth and the Trent & Mersey Canal (see p. 134). The river itself continues alongside the canal for some way, but this marks the limit of navigation.

The Sheffield & South Yorkshire Navigation

The navigation covers a composite of routes, starting with the Stainforth & Keadby Canal, passing on to the River Don and the Sheffield Canal. It is a fascinating mixture, with the flat Trent valley at one end and the rising hills of the Pennines at the other; artificial cutting alternates with natural river, industrial city with open countryside.

The first section of the route, along the Stainforth & Keadby, is the dullest, though there is an interesting device right at the beginning of the journey. Just beyond Keadby Lock the canal is crossed by a low railway bridge which has to be moved to allow boats to pass, but not by either lifting or swinging: this bridge slides sideways. Elsewhere along the route, swing bridges are the order of the day, providing welcome interruptions to the long straights. There is little to see, apart from the railway that keeps it company, but there is compensation in the abundant wild life on the water. The only town of any size is Thorne and here, at last, the canal abandons its unremitting straight line in favour of sweeping curves that enable it to follow the line of the Don valley. Beyond Bramwith Lock, the canal is joined by the New Junction Canal (see p. 80) and shortly after that the towers of Thorpe Marsh power station appear as vertical exclamation marks on the horizontal lines of this flat land.

The route now leads on to Doncaster, home of the St Leger, beyond which the canal gives way to the river. This area has been greatly improved in recent years by a major modernization scheme which has opened up the route to Rotherham to the big barges. It combines busy traffic with splendid scenery. At Sprotbrough, the river ducks under the viaduct to flow through a lovely wooded valley towards Conisbrough. The scenery changes again at Conisbrough, where there is a conflict between the old and the new – the ancient castle and the modern quarries. Here, too, is a quite magnificent railway viaduct, and it seems somewhat ironical that the old river navigation is still thriving while the railway is abandoned. Industry and open countryside alternate in the approach to Rotherham, with industry increasingly winning the battle. The huge Thrybergh Bar Mill marks the approach of Rotherham's forges and factories.

Rotherham also marks the end of river travel and the start of the Sheffield Canal, with 11 locks to lift the waterway from under the shadow of the M1 towards the steel city. The landscape is uncompromisingly industrial, but this is industry on a big scale and full of interest. The journey culminates in Sheffield Basin, a small piece of the industrial past preserved in the heart of the modern city. The old warehouses and the cobbled yards and wharves are all much as they were a century ago. Sheffield has changed, but here at least, at the end of the waterway, the old qualities of honest design in a working environment remain.

Below The Sheffield Basin.

Right A push-tow train on the Sheffield & South Yorkshire Navigation at Conisbrough.

The Aire & Calder Navigation

This is one of the earliest of the major river navigation schemes, though it has been much changed over the years and today can boast big, automated locks in place of the original small, manually-operated structures. It is approached from the Sheffield & South Yorkshire Navigation via the five-mile-long and dead straight New Junction Canal. Within that distance are one lock, one swing bridge and one short aqueduct. At the end of the canal, one can turn east towards Goole. This is very much a company town, developed around the docks that mark the junction between the Aire & Calder and the Ouse. The docks are still in use, and it is possible from here to travel on to Hull and the Humber or take a north-easterly route towards York (see p. 82). This section of the waterway carries a unique form of craft, the Tom Pudding. These square steel boxes, not unlike overgrown pudding tins, were introduced onto the Aire & Calder in 1862 and are still in use today. They each carry around 35 tons of coal and are hauled in convoy by a tug. At Goole, the Tom Puddings are picked out of the water by hydraulic hoists and their contents emptied into a waiting coaster.

The main line of the Aire & Calder runs west from the New Junction. It is a very wide canal with long straight sections interrupted only by locks and bridges. The landscape is mainly flat and, for many miles, all but deserted. There are few villages to tempt the traveller to stop – and mooring is, in any case, made difficult by the wash from the big barges and tankers. This is a busy waterway, and it is as well to keep clear of the heavy traffic. One possible stopping place is at Great Heck, where the basin offers safe mooring.

At Knottingley there is a junction where the river can be joined through Bank Dole Lock. It winds for five miles between high flood banks to the Selby Canal, which continues for four and a half miles to join the Ouse (see p. 82). The main canal passes through the small industrial town in a secluded cutting. This section is unusually narrow, and a one-way system operates, controlled by traffic lights. At the far end is Ferry-bridge Lock which leads out of the canal and down into the River Aire. Ferry-bridge itself has changed considerably in recent years. The elegant old bridge carrying the A1 has been replaced by a new, while the Ferrybridge power station offers no more than a reminder of the days when the barges queued to unload

their coal. The area is now dominated by collieries with their attendant flashes and spoil heaps. Then Castleford arrives and with it another junction. A short arm leads off into the town, the Calder joins the Aire, and a branch leads off to Wakefield. This branch is a mixture of natural river and artificial cutting which, until the end of 1982, still had a busy coal trade from Park Mill colliery. Now that is ended it is doubtful whether coal boats will ever be seen on the navigation again. There is one particularly interesting feature, the aqueduct – or rather aqueducts – at Stanley Ferry. River and canal part company at Woodnook Lock, and, by Stanley Ferry, the river has fallen so far below the level of the artificial cutting that the latter can cross over it. The aqueduct, completed in 1839, is unique, having the iron trough full of water suspended from two bow-string arches. It is no longer used and its modern replacement is more practical but somewhat less interesting. Wakefield itself is a pleasant town, its fine fourteenth-century bridge bearing a small chapel. Here the Aire & Calder joins the Calder & Hebble (see p. 101).

Back at Castleford, the main line continues westward towards Leeds through an area laid bare by mining and industrial waste. The river follows a wandering route, but the canal continues to head straight for its objective. The approach to the city offers a welcome change from the wasteland, with fine, tall warehouses lining the water. The route ends close to City Station, in the very heart of Leeds. It is a city well worth exploring, not least for its splendid Gothic town hall and its old shopping arcades. Those with no time to stop and stare can carry straight on into the Leeds & Liverpool Canal (see p. 92).

Right Commercial traffic at Ferrybridge with the power station in the background.

The Ouse (Yorkshire)

This is a river where the attraction lies not so much in the waterway itself as in the places to which it carries you – to Selby and York and to the edge of the Yorkshire Dales. The eastern end of the river is at Trent Falls, the confluence with the Trent, where the two rivers merge to become the Humber. The river is tidal as far as Naburn locks and these lower reaches can be vicious and dangerous. It can be joined with rather less nail biting above Goole, but still requires a good deal of care, for the river is used by coasters as far as Selby. This section does, however, provide access to the Derwent (see p. 84). The easiest approach to the river is via the Selby Canal. There is a further advantage in coming this way in that it avoids the dreary mud flats of the lower river and brings you straight into Selby. Once the river is reached there can still be problems, for this is still the tideway and it can prove decidedly tricky. The difficulties are well worth enduring for the pleasure of visiting Selby. This is a thriving town, full of character, with commerce in the shape of the riverside mills and warehouses sitting comfortably alongside its crowning glory, the twelfth-century abbey which has survived a whole series of catastrophes.

Although the river is tidal above Selby, its fierceness is considerably abated. The route continues to twist through flat, agricultural land, but there seems to be none of the bleakness that characterizes the route to the east. And the settlements along the way offer a great deal of variety and pleasure. Cawood is one of those villages built of mellow local brick which set this area of Yorkshire apart from the rest of the county. Of course, according to the new officialdom, Yorkshire no longer exists as an entity at all, but no Yorkshireman will ever accept that argument. A little beyond the village is the entrance to the River Wharfe (see p. 83). The Naburn locks appear, the tideway ends and the riverside scenery changes quite dramatically. Mud banks give way to meadows, trees creep up to hang their branches over the water and it is an altogether gentler stream that carries the traveller to York.

There is little to be said about York that has not been said in great length elsewhere. It is a city on which generations of invaders have left their mark, for both Norsemen and Romans settled here. It is a walled city, within which the intricate pattern of medieval streets can still be traced. It can boast, in its towering minster, one of the glories of European architecture. And, coming closer to the present day, it was the home of George Hudson, the railway king, and is

One of the many advantages of visiting York by water – it is far easier to find somewhere to moor a boat than it is to park a car.

now home to the National Railway Museum. But, it is also a city that built its prosperity on the river trade, and it has never turned its back on the river that gave it birth. There remains no better way to approach York than by water.

Above York, the river loses none of its charm. At Nun Monkton, the River Nidd joins the Ouse, but sadly is unnavigable. Here, too, the parkland of Beningbrough Hall reaches down to the water and stays as an accompaniment to Newton-on-Ouse. The scenery may be delightful, but navigation can be quite tricky due to a number of islets, many of which scarcely poke their noses above water. Beyond is Linton Lock, the last on the Ouse before it wanders off towards Swale Nab. This is the end of the Ouse, for above the confluence with the Swale it becomes the Ure – or, to put it more accurately, it is the combination of Ure and Swale that creates the Ouse. One's only regret is that the Swale itself is not navigable for, like the Nidd, it penetrates the Dale country. But although the Ouse has ended, the river journey is not yet complete, for boats can pass on without a pause into the Ure.

The Ure and the Ripon Canal/The Wharfe

The Ure and the Ripon Canal
The Ure, not surprisingly, offers very much the same sort of scenery as the Ouse, and with scenery such as this who would want a change? This is still the flat land of the Vale of York, but the hills of the Dales are beginning to make their presence felt. It offers peace and quiet, and even the towns have a tranquil air. Boroughbridge was once a busy main-road town and still boasts a number of coaching inns, but now it has been by-passed and left to its own devices. Here, too, one can find the Devil's Arrows, three strange, grooved stones of uncertain origin, said by legend to have been fired

Oxclose Lock at the junction of the River Ure and the Ripon Canal.

at Boroughbridge from the diabolic bow. Beyond that, the river is graced by the grounds of Newby Hall which lead up from the water's edge towards the house itself, one of the finest examples of the calm, classical style of Robert Adam.

The last stage of this journey deserts the river for the Ripon Canal. The whole canal is a mere two and a quarter miles long, with three locks, but the upper two are derelict, so the route stops short of Ripon itself. Plans are mooted for restoring this final stretch to give access to the delights of the market town. When that day arrives, boaters will be able to tie up within earshot of the Ripon Wakeman, who blows his horn each night in the square, as it has been blown for a thousand years.

The Wharfe
Upper Wharfedale can boast some of the finest of the famous Dale scenery that attracts so many visitors to Yorkshire. Those who set out to explore the river by boat are, sadly, in for something of a disappointment for travel is limited to a mere nine-mile run which has the characteristics of so many tidal rivers – a dull passage between muddy banks. Navigation ends at Tadcaster, where beer drinkers have their compensation. There are three breweries in the town – one modern, and two Smith breweries. John Smith's, with its ornate Victorian exterior, hides a remarkably modern plant, claiming the fastest canning line in Europe. Samuel Smith's is a traditional brewery producing traditional ale.

The Derwent

This is another fine navigation but sadly, at the time of writing, it is subject to dispute, a group of local landowners having claimed that there is no right of navigation over its waters. How the issue will be resolved there is no way of knowing, but it will be a sad day indeed if the river were to be closed to boats, particularly in view of the work put in by the Derwent Trust. They have already restored one of the five locks, in the hope of eventually bringing the river back to the status it enjoyed in 1701, when boats were first able to travel to Malton.

Entrance to the lower reaches is from the Ouse (see p. 82) and the Derwent is tidal for 15½ miles which can prove quite difficult, for the tides run high. Beyond that, however, the upper reaches have been said to offer the finest scenery of any navigable river in Britain – and it is hard to argue with that description. The through route was opened in 1972 with the restoration of Sutton Lock. Beyond that is Stamford Bridge, one of the few places of any size along the river. The serenity might have been disturbed by an inhabitant of Scrayingham graveyard, the railway entrepreneur George Hudson, but he never brought his tracks to this part of the Derwent valley. There are not many boats to disturb the peace either, for nearby Buttercrambe Lock is unusable. The rest of the river, and the best of the river, lies tantalizingly out of reach. No boats can pass by the ruins of Kirkham Priory, or pass the great pile of Castle Howard to the quiet town of Malton. One can only hope that this will not always be so.

One short canal runs off the Derwent at East Cottingwith, the Pocklington, a waterway on which restoration work is well in hand. It is hoped to restore the whole nine and a half miles, which will include the rebuilding of seven locks and three swing bridges. At present the canal is navigable for four and a half miles from the junction, enough to get a taste for the canal and a wish to see the rest. It is a pleasant, quiet, remote, wandering sort of affair, skirting round villages and never even reaching Pocklington itself. The route stops at Canal Head by the A1079, south of the town. The pleasures of this waterway tend to be small-scale, but lovers of canal architecture will revel in the sinuous curves and rich colouring of its brick bridges.

Left The guillotine lock at Sutton-on-Derwent, rebuilt in 1972 when the waterway was reopened.

Above Stamford Bridge. The elegant eighteenth-century bridge stands near the site where Harold defeated the Danes in 1066.

The Ancholme

This is not a river that is much visited by cruising enthusiasts, largely because the only access is from the wide reaches of the Humber. The river itself is peaceful enough, protected from the tides by the lock at South Ferriby. This is also the home of the last survivor of a class of boat that was once common on the rivers and canals of the region, the Humber sloop, *Amy Howson*. Her sister ship, the square-rigged keel, *Comrade*, is berthed across the Humber at Hull. Both are sailed regularly.

The river itself is canalized, running in long straights through an area of flat countryside aptly named New Holland. The one town along the way is Brigg, where the river divides into two navigable loops – a sort of waterways ring road. Here is some of the best of the river scenery, with secluded, wooded sections. For most travellers, journey's end is Harlam Hill Lock. There is a further two miles of navigable river beyond this point, but the lock takes an incredible four hours to operate, so it is far simpler and quicker to walk.

A sailing boat leaving South Ferriby.

The Hull and the Driffield Navigation

The River Hull in the centre of Hull itself presents the busiest river scene to be found in Britain, with big barges passing up and down a channel made narrow by other barges, moored as many as six deep. Entrance to the river from the Humber is under the huge flood barrier, and, like all tidal rivers with a busy commercial traffic, the Hull should be avoided by all but the most experienced. The keel *Comrade* is usually to be found here, easily spotted by the tall mast rising above the barges. There are no moorings for pleasure craft, which should head straight on to Beverley Beck, 11 miles upstream. The Beck offers safe moorings and a chance to explore this lovely town with its magnificent Gothic minster and Regency terraces. Back on the river, progress continues to be difficult, the scenery continues to be drab and there is little change until Struncheon Hill Lock is reached and the entrance to the Driffield Navigation.

Restorers are already hard at work on

A motorized barge at Hull Bridge.

this derelict canal, and there is every hope that it will be open to traffic before long. There are seven locks, and seven miles of pleasant waterway leading up to Driffield itself, where the old warehouses round the canal basin have been imaginatively converted into flats. The navigation also boasts its own unique type of sailing boat, a lug-sailed dinghy, the Brigham Scow.

The Chesterfield Canal/The Idle

Of the two navigations leaving the Trent at West Stockwith, the Idle is by far the duller. Entry is under a single guillotine gate, and once on the river there is little to be seen apart from the high mud banks. Few come this way, and it is not hard to see why. Navigation ends at Bawtry which, before it was bypassed, was a busy coaching stop on the Great North Road. Now the coaching inn is the only reminder of those busy days.

The second of the routes off the Trent could certainly never be described as dull. The Chesterfield Canal is, in fact, a remarkably beautiful canal, which appears all the more remarkable if one has just turned into it from the wide, fast-flowing Trent. In contrast to the open spaces of the river, here is a waterway which occupies a very secluded, private little world all of its own.

The canal begins at West Stockwith Basin, from where it runs straight on for one mile to the first of two broad locks at Misterton. This is one of the few straight sections on what is, in general, precisely the sort of twisting canal that one might expect on hearing that it was started under the direction of James Brindley. The line is dictated by the presence of the Gringley hills, towards which the canal wriggles off and then wanders round, following the contours of the northern slopes. As with so many early canals, the effect of all this wandering is to give the boater time in plenty to relax and enjoy the scenery. Eventually, the low hills begin to close in and a sharp bend leads to a deep, wooded cutting, culminating in a 154-yard tunnel.

On the far side of Drakeholes Tunnel one comes out into the sheltered and, one hopes, sunny southern flank of the hills. The canal now seems, if anything, even more remote and peaceful, as it skirts the parkland of Wiseton, passes the Retford & Worksop Boat Club and nine miles of beautiful, uninterrupted cruising ends at Whitsunday Pie Lock. The name dates back to the time when the lock was being built, when a kindly farmer's wife brought out a huge pork pie on Whit Sunday for the navvies. Retford, a quiet market town, is soon reached, and seems especially quiet when seen from the canal which takes a very pleasing route through it. Here the broad locks give way to conventional narrow locks, but there is no fundamental change in the scenery which, if anything, becomes even more attractive. Woodland and open country alternate, the peace only briefly disturbed by the arrival of the A1. Once that is left behind, the canal follows the Ryton valley to Scofton and the superb parkland of Osberton Hall.

The last stretch of canal runs into Worksop, under a warehouse arched over the waterway and once used by Pickfords, the furniture removal firm which began life as canal carriers. The route comes to an abrupt conclusion at derelict Morse Lock. Originally it continued for another 19½ miles to Chesterfield, and a local group is, at present, busily working on restoration plans. The derelict section contains many problems, including a row of houses built over the original line! However, the section above Worksop is every bit as attractive as the rest, so any extension of this most beautiful canal would be warmly welcomed.

Left An old warehouse at Worksop on the Chesterfield.

Right Drakeholes Tunnel.

The North-West

This region offers some of the most dramatic waterway scenery in Britain, dominated as it is by the Pennine hills. It also offers some of the greatest contrasts, with cities and mill towns alternating with open moorland. All these facets can be seen in the canal that could be said to exemplify the whole area, the Leeds & Liverpool, the major route to traverse the Pennines and the longest canal in Britain. There are two other trans-Pennine routes, each offering some spectacular scenery and both are currently undergoing restoration. One Yorkshire canal has been allowed to creep in, primarily because it forms a link in the trans-Pennine system.

A second main group consists of the waterways centred on Manchester, including the only waterway to be constructed in the late nineteenth century, the Manchester Ship Canal. That leaves just two isolated sections: one, the Lancaster Canal, because its links with the rest of the system have long since been severed, while the second, the Lakes, is isolated by nature.

The Leeds & Liverpool Canal

The Bridgewater Canal

The Rochdale Canal

The Ashton Canal

The Peak Forest Canal

The Macclesfield Canal

The Huddersfield Canals

The Calder & Hebble Navigation

The Manchester Ship Canal

The St Helen's Canal

The Lancaster Canal

The Lake District

Windemere

Kendal

N

0 5 10 15 20 miles
0 5 10 15 20 25 km

Carnforth

Morecambe

Lancaster

LANCASTER

Glasson

Harrogate

Skipton

Kildwick

Garstang

Barnoldswick

Keighley

Leeds

Catterall

Foulridge

LEEDS & LIVERPOOL

Haworth

Bingley
Saltaire

Kirkstall

Blackpool

Preston

Nelson

Burnley

Bradford

Hebden
Bridge

Halifax

Brighouse

Dewsbury

Blackburn

Todmorden

Sowerby
Bridge

Cooper
Bridge

CALDER & HEBBLE

ROCHDALE

BROAD

Chorley

Rochdale

Littleborough

Huddersfield

Rufford

RUFFORD

Bolton

Bury

HUDDERSFIELD NARROW

Burscough

Parbold

LEEDS & LIVERPOOL

Wigan

Barnsley

Leigh

Worsley

Barton swing
aqueduct

Ashton

Dukinfield

ST HELENS

LEIGH

MANCHESTER SHIP

BRIDGEWATER

PEAK FOREST

Manchester

Sheffield

Warrington

Liverpool

Sankey

Lymm

Grappenhall

Marple

Bugsworth

BUXWORTH ?

Runcorn

Eastham

Weston

Preston Brook

Whaley Bridge

Bollington

Ellesmere Port
Ellesmere Port

WEAVER

MACCLESFIELD

Macclesfield

DEE

SHROPSHIRE   UNION

Congleton

Crewe

Mow Cop

Stoke

91

The Leeds & Liverpool Canal

The longest canal in Britain, the Leeds & Liverpool also took the longest time to complete. Work began in 1770, and the whole route was at last finished in 1816. The delays were caused less by engineering problems than by that other perennial headache of canal builders – shortage of cash. Work stopped and started, engineers came and went, and one would expect to find evidence of the many different hands and minds involved in a mixture of styles along the way. Yet this is not the case at all. Indeed, for such a long route, it has a remarkable homogeneity of character, which is not at all the same thing as saying that it suffers from uniformity, in the sense of dullness: far from it. Indeed, one of the first things one notices about the Leeds & Liverpool is that it does things very much its own way, with scant regard for other canal methods and styles. For a start, except for the Leigh branch and the section from Wigan to Liverpool the dimensions of the locks make it unusable by the narrow boats of the Midlands. Elsewhere, although there is ample width in the locks for two narrow boats, the maximum length of boat is only 60 feet. So the canal developed its very own type of vessel, the short boat. Individuality also appears in the working of the locks. There are the familiar paddles to be wound up by windlass, but there are also 'Jack cloughs'. In these, the paddles are swung across the face of the culvert by levering on a long, wooden handle. These incidentals add variety to a canal which might already be thought to have more than its fair share of interesting features.

The canal begins at the Leeds end at a junction with the Aire & Calder (see p. 80) and continues to follow the River Aire westwards. The beginning is very much a city centre affair, and at first it is the old Leeds of woollen mills and factories that dominates the scene. In fact, at Bridge 225 the canal runs past Armley Mill, founded by Benjamin Gott, the pioneer of steam power and mechanization in the wool industry. Appropriately enough, this is now home to a new industrial museum. Six locks lift the canal out of the city, and quite quickly the impact of the urban industrial scene begins to diminish while at Kirkstall there is a reminder, in the ruins of the twelfth-century abbey, that Leeds was important long before Mr Gott and his friends appeared on the scene. The smoke-blackened walls, however, show where Gott and co. left their marks. Here, the route, though still close to Leeds, seems positively rural, mainly because it sticks so close to the river valley. Hills and trees close it off from the city suburbs as it continues its steady climb up Airedale. Not that there is

always a great deal of time for viewing the scenery, for even when there are no locks to work, there is never a shortage of those other great features of the route – low bridges which have to be swung out of the way by hand. Some move with ease; others seem to require the concerted shove of a pack of Rugby forwards.

The canal skirts round the edge of Shipley to arrive at the village of Saltaire, which amply repays a little time spent at moorings. The principal feature seen from the canal is the vast nineteenth-century mill straddling the water. This was built by Sir Titus Salt, manufacturer of mohair, who gave his name to the village. He was a mayor of Bradford who, during his mayoralty, was so shocked by the conditions in the city that he built a model town for his mill workers. The town has scarcely changed, and how fine it is with good housing, hospital, alms houses, church and library – everything the community needed, with one exception. Salt, a tee-totaller, decreed that there should be no pub.

After the spectacular mill comes the waterway's own spectacular, as it charges up the hill in ever-increasing leaps – first a single lock, then two locks and at Bingley two last great leaps, the three- and five-lock staircases. It is the latter that offers the spectacle, five inter-connected locks, lifting the canal 60 feet. Using the staircase can result in a good deal of head scratching and puzzlement. Coming downhill is no problem. You simply enter the top lock, and the water from that will flow into the one below and so on. Uphill travel is not so simple. You cannot fill the lock you are in unless there is water in the lock above, so it is necessary to push water down from the top before you can begin the uphill journey. A lock keeper is generally on hand and a notice board at the top provides the necessary instructions, though some might find those instructions more confusing than helpful. Common sense is the greatest help in these circumstances. The locks must, however, be treated gently. Filling a lock from such a height results in a cascade of water which can swamp the unwary. Take care and you will be rewarded by one of the great experiences of canal travel, the climb up the celebrated Bingley five-rise locks.

Left The church and mill built by Sir Titus Salt at Saltaire.

Below The great five-rise locks at Bingley.

The Leeds & Liverpool Canal

The reward for all that endeavour comes in the form of 17 miles with no locks at all – but not, alas, equally devoid of swing bridges. It also marks the beginning of a distinct change in the character of the canal, for the world of the wool towns is gradually left behind for the open country and the moorland. At first, the route follows the shoulder of the hill above the Aire, so that there are wide views across the valley to the industrial towns signposted by the mill chimney pointers. A mile from the canal is Keighley, starting point for the Keighley & Worth Valley Railway, the line made famous by the film *The Railway Children*. It wanders off to Haworth and Brontë country, while the canal takes a no less splendid route – better, in fact, in some ways since the villages have escaped Brontëization and are spared the Wuthering Heights Gifte Shoppes. At Kildwick, for example, the Old Hall sits somewhat dourly above the water, while the village houses stand with their backs to the canal which laps at their stone walls. It is not a conventionally pretty village in the way that a Somerset village might be called pretty, but it is a place that is completely at home in this landscape. The first town is Skipton, made up of a rich mixture of ingredients. The first sight from the canal is very much related to that aspect that gave the town its name, the Saxon 'Sheep Town'. Stone woollen mills line the waterway and the wharves. Beyond them is the market square and the splendid castle, which is bordered by a short arm of the canal. It is a lovely, mellow town, often known as the gateway to the Dales and so, in canal terms, it is.

Beyond Skipton the canal makes its way along the upper levels of Airedale, with the hills getting nearer, until the six Bank Newton locks appear to lift the waterway to its summit level. Scenically, this is perhaps the best of a fine route. Here the canal has penetrated to the heart of the Pennines, through which it can only make its way by a series of great sweeping bends. The moorland rises steeply round the canal. The straggling dry stone walls, the grazing sheep and the few trees leaning in the wind complete the typical Pennine scene. It would be a disappointment when the section ends, did it not end in such a lovely flight of locks as that at Greenberfield. Happily, there is still plenty of splendid scenery to come, as the canal passes on to Barnoldswick – pronounced 'Barlick' by the locals – and Foulridge.

Here the view disappears altogether as the canal dives into the 1640-yard-long tunnel. Foulridge itself makes a pleasant stopping-off place, as the cow could have testified in 1912 when it swam right through the tunnel and was revived here by a pint of the best.

Foulridge marks a definite divide in the canal, for beyond it are the Barrowford locks which lead on to the cotton towns of Lancashire, through Nelson to Burnley. Here one finds another of those features that make this canal special – the Burnley Mile, an embankment that rises high above the town. It used to be said that it offered the finest view of an industrial landscape in Britain, but much has changed in recent years. Now the best landscape is found at the end of the mile, as the canal swings round into the area known as the Weavers' Triangle. Here the tall mills and warehouses are built of the local stone, harmonizing in their own rough and rugged way with the surrounding hills.

The canal sets up a rhythm of its own, open hill country and moorland alternating with the mill towns. Blackburn is perhaps the most interesting of the latter, for the canal takes a route high above the town looking down on the great Victorian mills, before reaching the older mills that cluster round the little flight of locks. And the section beyond Blackburn offers some of the best of the hill scenery, culminating in the totally delightful flight of locks at Johnson's Hillocks. The rhythm is finally broken at Wigan, where the canal bids its farewell

to the Pennines, clambering down through 21 locks. These certainly offer more than their share of hard work, for as well as the normal problems of lock working, these are padlocked to avoid vandalism, so that they all have to be locked and unlocked by a special key provided by the B.W.B. At the bottom is the Leigh Branch, which leads away south to connect with the Bridgewater Canal (see p. 96), and the basin with the famous Wigan Pier. The pier does exist, even if it is no more than a scarcely discernible bump on the wharf, but the basin itself is a splendid example of an early canal and industrial complex.

The route westward from Wigan is comparatively little used. Most pleasure boaters prefer the drama of the Pennines to the flat lands of the coastal plain. Yet, once one has accepted that the grandeur is over, the journey down the Douglas valley proves to be very attractive. The valley itself is wooded and peaceful, apart from the occasional train on the adjoining railway. Gradually, however, it begins to open out as the views get ever wider and the land steadily flatter. Some attractive villages appear, notably Parbold, where the stump of the old windmill makes a prominent landmark. At Burscough, the Rufford Arm leads away, a quiet, pleasant route with eight locks in seven miles, taking boats down to the Douglas and the Ribble estuary.

Open countryside comes to an end on the outskirts of Liverpool, at a spot known to millions who know there is a canal here but have no idea which canal. For this is Aintree, home of the Grand National, where the race course meets the canal and bends away at the canal turn. Now Liverpool begins to assert itself. The canal takes a route parallel to the Mersey, which remains largely out of sight behind high dock walls. A short flight of locks eventually leads down to Stanley Dock, while the main line runs on to an abrupt end at Chisenhale Bridge. The canal that begins among the woollen mills of Yorkshire and runs on through the cotton towns of Lancashire concludes here at the port that grew with the Industrial Revolution. It is no longer the international giant that it was a century ago, but Liverpool still carries the badges of its former greatness in the shape of some of the finest architecture in Britain and a new and very impressive Maritime Museum.

Left Greenberfield locks in the heart of the Pennines.

Above The Leeds & Liverpool at Liverpool.

The Bridgewater Canal

Approaching the Bridgewater from the north via the Leigh Branch of the Leeds & Liverpool, there is very little to indicate that you have left the one and arrived at the other. Six miles of travel through a strange and bare landscape of spoil heaps and mining flashes bring one to a spot famous in canal history – Worsley. It was here that the Duke of Bridgewater made his home and here that he had his mine, Worsley Delph. The mine entrance can be seen across the main road from Worsley Basin, the canal emerging from its depths, stained an unlikely orange by ore in the workings. The basin is an attractive spot, a picturesque group of black and white timbered buildings surviving under the shadow of the M62.

Two miles beyond Worsley is the Barton swing aqueduct, which carries the canal across the Manchester Ship Canal. The water is carried in an iron trough which pivots on a central island, and it can either be set to allow boats to pass down the Bridgewater, or the ends can be closed and the whole trough full of water swung out of the way to allow the bigger ships to pass underneath. Even if it is set for boats on the Bridgewater, it is worth while waiting to see if it is to be swung, for it is a remarkable sight. From here the route leads on to Manchester, which has its share of interest and surprises. This inland waterway to an inland city seems suddenly to reach the sea, for across a wharf area can be seen the tall masts and funnels of cargo ships. In fact, the Bridgewater runs alongside the dock complex in Manchester, the end of the Ship Canal. It is possible to join the Ship Canal or move on to the junction with the Rochdale Canal (see p. 97) and on through the centre of Manchester. The canal also arrives at the back of the old Liverpool & Manchester Railway Station, the first purpose-built station in the world, now home to an industrial museum.

As an alternative to travelling through Manchester, the main line of the Bridgewater can be followed south-west towards Runcorn. This is an ideal canal for the strictly non-energetic boater, for it is lock free for 28 pleasant miles.

Inevitably, the first few miles are urban and industrial. Manchester was one of the great growth cities of the Industrial Revolution, and this now peaceful canal played a major role in that growth. Soon, however, open country is reached and there are some more of those surprising views across to the Ship Canal, providing an illusion of ships making a mysterious progress across ploughed fields. There are pleasant villages, Lymm and Grappenhall, and far more variety in the scenery than one might expect in such a flat landscape. At Preston Brook, an important canal junction town in its day, the Bridgewater meets the Trent & Mersey (see p. 134), then continues for another five miles to Runcorn. Once it was connected to the Mersey by a flight of locks, but these are now derelict and everything comes to an abrupt halt at Waterloo Bridge. The Bridgewater has, in recent years, become more popular as part of the Cheshire Ring of waterways and certainly, with its rich historical associations, it well deserves its popularity.

Worsley Basin near Manchester.

The Rochdale Canal

The summit level in the heart of the Pennines.

Apart from its many other qualities, the Rochdale Canal represents a major feat of engineering. Where the earlier east-west route, the Leeds & Liverpool, had skirted round the worst of the Pennine hills, the Rochdale was pushed through extraordinarily difficult country. Sadly, only· one short section is currently navigable, but restoration work is well in hand on other sections – and even if boats can no longer pass over its waters, feet can use its towpath.

The navigable section, which is our main concern here, links the Bridge-water Canal to the Ashton. There is only a mile of canal and a mere nine locks, but what an enthralling mile it turns out to be. The canal is shut away behind high walls, but beyond those walls one can see the Byzantine splendour of the old commercial centre of Manchester, offices and warehouses, rich with archi-tectural embellishment. Then, right at the top, the whole waterway disappears from view beneath a modern tower block and there in the dark, between the foundation pillars of the building, is what must be the gloomiest lock in Britain. Emerging again into the daylight, one is faced with the last lock and the Canal Company offices, for the Rochdale is still privately owned. Navigation now continues on the Ashton Canal, but the Rochdale itself continues eastwards.

The rest of the canal is like the Leeds & Liverpool in so far as there is a steady alternation of mill towns and open country. Visually, however, the effect is quite different, for the Rochdale follows the narrow Roch valley, hemmed in by steeply rising moors. The wild sections, such as that between Littleborough and Todmorden, are quite splendid, with a real feeling of wilderness about them. And the towns are scarcely less im-pressive. At Hebden Bridge, for ex-ample, where the river is crossed on a short aqueduct, the whole story of the industrial past of the Pennines is written on the land. High on the hill stands the ancient village of Heptonstall, once a weaving centre. The pack-horse route then leads down to Hebden, where both river and canal are lined with mills, with the houses ranged in lofty terraces up the hillside. The canal route ends at Sowerby Bridge, the junction with the Calder & Hebble (see p. 101). Along the way, the difficult terrain has been conquered by building 92 locks in 33 miles. When the Rochdale is finally reopened to traffic it will be hard work for boaters, but in-finitely worth the effort.

The Ashton/The Peak Forest/Macclesfield Canals

The Ashton Canal

This is a short canal but an important one, forming a vital link between Manchester and the other canals of the North West and forming a part of the Cheshire Ring. It is just under seven miles long with 18 locks and is completely urban throughout its length. It starts at Ducie Street at a junction with the navigable Rochdale, then climbs up steadily between mills and warehouses to Dukinfield and a junction with the Peak Forest Canal. The main line continues on for a further half-mile to join the unnavigable Huddersfield Canal (see p. 100). It is one of the country's successful restoration schemes: those who enjoy its Lowry-esque landscape will pause to admire; others will hurry on through.

The Peak Forest Canal

There is a wealth of variety and interest crammed into this one short canal. It has everything, starting with the most urban of urban beginnings, to open hillsides, and can boast two tunnels, a splendid flight of locks, a quite magnificent aqueduct and, at the end of the journey, a unique canal-railway interchange.

The beginning at Dukinfield gives little indication of what lies ahead, for the surroundings are still very much those of outer Manchester. It soon begins to open out, however, with cotton mills dotting the route to Hyde Bank Tunnel. This is something of a curiosity, with an elliptically arched opening and a decided kink in the middle. Beyond that, the canal has its finest moment with the crossing of the River Goyt on a three-arched stone aqueduct, which stands almost 100 feet above the river. It is not just the aqueduct that is impressive, for the scenery matches it for grandeur, the river flowing between steep, wooded banks. After that, work begins. The 16 locks of the Marple flight add to the mixture, beginning in open country and ending at the town centre at the junction with the Macclesfield Canal (see below) which forms the next link in the Cheshire Ring.

The Peak Forest continues, however, for another six and a half miles to Whaley Bridge and it is a detour well worth making. The beginning, in particular, is spectacular, as the canal swings round to follow a high-level route above the Goyt valley. It is lock free, but not free from swing bridges which can prove uncomfortably unswingable. At Whaley Bridge the canal ends abruptly in the interchange shed. Boats used to float in at one end, unload and return, while the cargo was then loaded onto the waggons of the Cromfort & High Peak Railway, whose rails ran from the opposite end of the shed. Originally the main line ended at the fascinating complex of Bugsworth Basin. As with the Ashton, the route can only be travelled today thanks to the efforts of volunteer restorers.

The Macclesfield Canal

The Macclesfield Canal, which completes the Cheshire Ring by joining the Peak Forest to the Trent & Mersey, only just made it into the canal world. Work began in 1825, and there was much discussion as to whether or not a railway might be a better notion. In strictly financial terms, the railway might well have been a better bet, but canal lovers must all be grateful that the decision went the other way. There are few who travel this canal who do not at once vote it as among their favourites.

One factor that dignifies the canal appears at the beginning, the magnificent masonry work of its many bridges. The so-called 'snake bridges', in particular, must rank among the most beautiful structures to be found on any canal. They were designed to fulfil a common canal function, to carry the towpath from one side of the waterway to the other, but in such a way that the towrope would not need to be unhitched from the horse. To achieve this, the bridges coil round for the ramp to come back under the arch.

Leaving Marple, the canal takes a high-level route through the hill country that is so characteristic of the whole waterway. Towns are few and come in for very different treatments. At Bollington, the canal rears up high over the little stone-built town, crossing the main road on a high aqueduct, while at Macclesfield the town is scarcely seen at all, for the canal spends much of its time lurking in a deep cutting. Congleton, next in line, is skirted round, the road again being crossed by an aqueduct, this time a handsome affair in ornate cast iron. Here too, at either end of the aqueduct, are the best pair of snake bridges.

Beyond Congleton, the canal scarcely touches habitation, offering wide views across to the hills until Bosley locks arrive, a flight of 12 to carry boats down from the upper level to the Dane valley. But there are still delights to come as the canal laps the lawns of Ramsdell Hall, while offering views across to that most extraordinary of black and white buildings, Little Moreton Hall and the equally remarkable folly of Mow Cop. It all ends with an aquatic flyover, as the Macclesfield crosses over the Trent & Mersey, runs parallel with it for a while and then joins it (see p. 134).

Below The 'snake bridge' near Congleton on the Macclesfield Canal.

Right The Marple Aqueduct.

The Huddersfield Canals

The extraordinary Huddersfield Narrow Canal provides the third option for those wanting to cross the Pennines – or will do so when restoration work is complete. It also offered the working boatman of the old days quite the hardest labour of any canal in Britain. Not only were there 74 locks in less than 20 miles, but the canal also boasts the longest tunnel, three miles and 135 yards with no towpath. The only way to get through in the days of horse boats was by legging, and things got even worse when the railways came, for the railway tunnel and the canal tunnel shared the same ventilation system. Whenever a train came through,

both tunnels filled with the smoke. Why, then, one might ask, should anyone want to restore such a route? There are two answers. First it is by far the shortest route through the Pennines, and secondly it is a canal which mixes mill and moorland again, but in quite a different way. It also has the highest summit level of any British canal, 638 feet above sea level.

At present, the canal is unnavigable, but restoration work has begun, and the towpath can be walked on either side of the tunnel. Perhaps the most exhilarating feature of this canal is the way in which it passes through such heavily

industrialized areas yet still manages to capture and hold the atmosphere of the surrounding hills. It is equally appealing to those who love the wild scenery of the Pennines and to those who are intrigued by industrial history.

At Huddersfield itself it gives way to the short Huddersfield Broad Canal. This is still navigable and connects with the Calder & Hebble Navigation at Cooper Bridge.

A unique lifting bridge at Huddersfield.

The Calder & Hebble Navigation

The Calder & Hebble, a river navigation which alternates river travel with artificial cuttings, joins the Rochdale Canal (see p. 97) to the Aire & Calder (see p. 80). The start at Sowerby Bridge is quite splendid: the old warehouses that served the Calder & Hebble and the Rochdale could be taken as models of the argument in favour of the plain functional style combined with natural materials. This is the highest point on the route, and the presence of the surrounding hills is very much felt as the canal follows the Calder valley round Halifax. It is a shame that the canal does not come rather closer to the city centre for Halifax has much to offer, including the superb and recently renovated Piece Hall, where wool merchants came to trade. By way of compensation, the canal does enter one of its most attractive reaches, with wooded cliffs overhanging the water. Then it begins to drop down until, at the attractive market town of Brighouse, canal and river meet, and boats leave the artificial waterway for the wooded river valley. The route must once have seemed remote from civilization, but now it has the railway, with some very impressive viaducts, for company, and is crossed by the M62.

On the rest of the journey, river and canal continue to alternate, but the scenery becomes steadily more urban and industrialized. This is very much an area that owes its character to the twin influences of mining and wool. If descriptions such as charming and pretty would be entirely out of place, others such as honest and rugged seem altogether applicable. Even if the landscape does not suit all tastes, the canal itself has a good deal to offer in the form of canalside buildings of local stone that seem not so much to have been built as to have grown directly from the land. The Huddersfield Broad Canal leads off westward at Cooper Bridge, as the main line continues on to Wakefield and the Aire & Calder.

Above The canal near Elland.

Below The basin and warehouses of Sowerby Bridge are now home to a holiday hire boat fleet.

The Manchester Ship Canal/The St Helens Canal

The Manchester Ship Canal

Of all the inland waterways that one is unlikely to travel in a conventional pleasure craft, this must be at the head of the list. It was built at the end of the nineteenth century to take deep-sea cargo vessels from the tidal River Mersey at Eastham up to a new port complex in Manchester, and it still fulfils that function today. Not surprisingly, the authorities are not especially keen on allowing pleasure craft on their waters, and those that are allowed on are admitted only under the strictest rules. But if one is unlikely to travel the ship canal, one is very likely to come across it at one of the points where it is joined by other navigations – by the Shropshire Union at Ellesmere Port (see p. 109) or the Weaver at Weston Point (see p. 108). It is in any case an interesting canal, the most ambitious ever built in Britain, the last great flourish of the canal age. Everything about it is on a colossal scale, from the 600-feet-long lock at Eastham to the docks in Manchester. It is grand, impressive, but quite definitely not for the average holiday boater.

The St Helens Canal

Originally known as the Sankey Brook, this is said by many to be the first canal in mainland Britain (it was opened in 1757), and is thus of considerable historical interest. Until very recently it was entirely derelict, but part has now been opened up so that vessels from the Mersey can reach Fiddler's Ferry power station. It is unlikely ever to be of great interest to pleasure boaters, but there is one place on the canal that will always fascinate those who care about transport history. At Sankey this pioneering waterway is crossed by a viaduct, designed by George Stephenson to carry his equally innovatory Liverpool & Manchester Railway.

Right The Barton Swing Aqueduct takes the Bridgewater Canal over the Manchester Ship Canal.

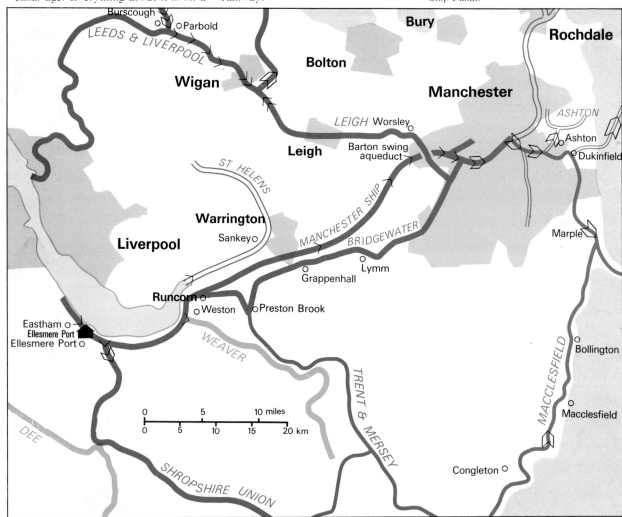

The Lancaster Canal/The Lake District

The Lancaster Canal

The Lancaster was once integrated into the rest of the system, but has now been severed, its only link being down to the sea. Apart from losing its connection at the southern end, the canal suffered a major amputation at the northern end, when 14 miles were lopped off its length. Nevertheless, what remains has a good deal to offer, including an especially fine aqueduct.

Navigation starts at the southern end, at Preston, at one of those nondescript points that show quite clearly that it was not the original starting point. In fact, it once connected right through to the Leeds & Liverpool. The first part of the canal runs through a very flat, but far from dull, landscape, and the canal itself has a good deal to offer: the stone bridges are exceptionally elegant, and as a canal it can rival the Macclesfield for the excellence of its masonry work. The next features of note are the aqueducts – not the conventional ones, we shall come to those later – but those which use unusual means to cross the rivers that lie in its path. At Catterall, for example, is the first of the siphon aqueducts, where instead of lifting the canal over the river, the engineer, John Rennie, diverted the river under the canal, siphoning it through a giant U-tube.

Travelling the Lancaster is a pleasantly undemanding sort of occupation. There are no locks on the main line, and the countryside is pleasantly agricultural, with little to disturb the serenity apart from the occasional train on the nearby Glasgow main line – and the M6, the villain of the Lancaster story. At this point, however, the motorway is no more than an occasional visitor. The canal continues its placid way to Garstang, a pleasant little town with a cobbled market square. By now, the hills are starting to make an impact on the landscape as a distant backdrop.

Another eight miles lead to the turn to the Glasson Avon which goes down via six locks to Glasson Basin and the tidal River Lune. It makes a pleasant diversion, especially for those who are suffering lock deprivation.

The main line continues on to Lancaster, a town dominated by the huge Ashton Memorial. Here the canal has its finest moments. The passage through the town is full of interest with old wharves and warehouses and many reminders that Lancaster was once a busy port. It culminates in the crossing of the River Lune by a 600-feet-long aqueduct. This was Rennie's masterpiece, greater in scale than the well-known aqueducts on the Kennet & Avon and every bit as handsome. After that the canal wanders off for a look at the sea at Hest Bank, with views across Morecambe Bay, before cutting back inland to Carnforth.

Above The Lune Aqueduct.

Right Cruising on the Glasson Arm of the Lancaster Canal.

Ahead, tantalizingly, are the hills of the Lake District but, sadly, journey's end is near. A winding section leads to the derelict locks at Tewitfield, at the top of which is that villainous M6, its high embankment running right across the line of the canal. Beyond it, the unused canal carries on to Kendal. But if the Lancaster Canal is not quite what it was, its isolation has at least ensured that this pleasant waterway has remained a peaceful one.

The Lake District

This is not, perhaps, a cruising area in that there is little opportunity for continuous boating. Hire boats are available on the larger lakes, but as even the largest of them, Windermere, is just over ten miles long, scope is somewhat limited. Windermere, Ullswater and Coniston also have passenger boats, and the hire boats can be used for a day's pottering around. The Lakes have been popular with potterers for more than a century, and the elegant days of Victorian and Edwardian boating are remembered in the collection of launches at the Windermere Steamboat Museum and in the restored 1859 steam yacht *Gondola* which gives passenger trips on Coniston.

The West Midlands

This region could be taken as a model to show why and how the canal system of Britain was developed. It is bounded on three sides by rivers – the Mersey, the Severn and the Avon, while at the centre of the fourth side stands land-locked Birmingham with no natural access to the sea. The rivers have been used for trade for centuries, but it was not until the eighteenth century that they were joined to each other by the web of canals, and to the developing industrial Midlands. Canal building in the region covers the whole spectrum, from the meandering line of Brindley's Staffordshire & Worcestershire Canal to the straight lines of Telford's Birmingham & Liverpool Junction. Today, the region can offer the full range of boating pleasures: rural idylls or urban explorations: quiet, small-scale pleasures or the most amazing boat trip to be had on the inland waterways. There are wide rivers and narrow canals to choose between and, at the beginning of this section, we shall look at a waterway which is unlike the rest in still carrying large-scale commercial traffic, and which can boast one extraordinary example of Victorian engineering – The Weaver.

The Weaver

The Shropshire Union

The Dee

The Llangollen Canal

The Montgomery Canal

The Severn

The Avon

The Stratford-upon-Avon Canal

The Worcester & Birmingham Canal

The Staffordshire & Worcestershire Canal

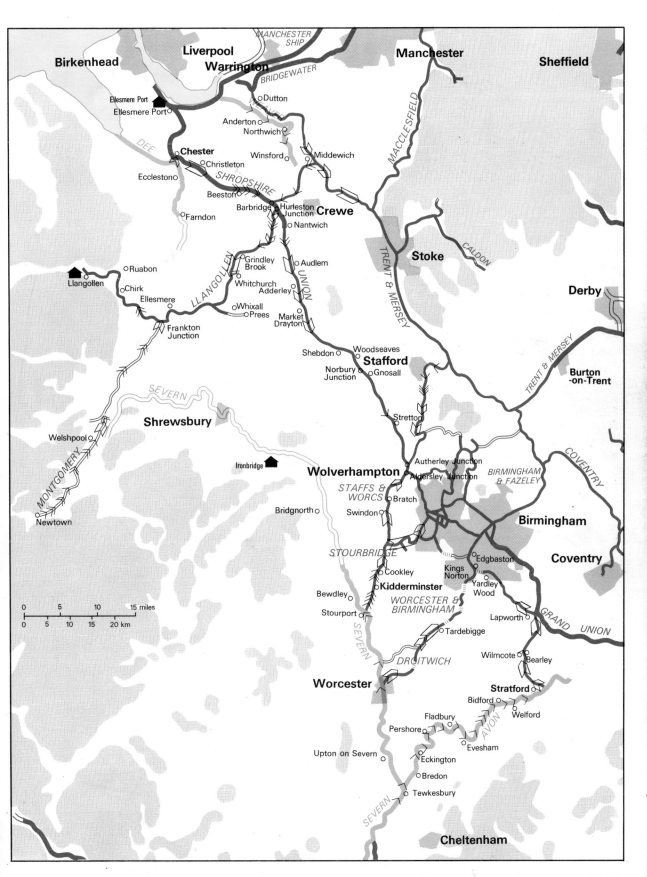

Birkenhead

Liverpool
Warrington

Manchester

Sheffield

MANCHESTER SHIP

BRIDGEWATER

Ellesmere Port
Ellesmere Port

Dutton

MACCLESFIELD

DEE

Anderton
Northwich

Chester
Christleton

Eccleston

Winsford

Middewich

SHROPSHIRE

Beeston

Barbridge

Hurleston
Junction

Crewe

Farndon

Nantwich

Stoke

CALDON

Ruabon

Grindley
Brook

Audlem

Llangollen

Chirk

Ellesmere

LLANGOLLEN

Whitchurch
Adderley

UNION

Derby

TRENT & MERSEY

Whixall
Prees

Market
Drayton

Frankton
Junction

Shebdon

Woodseaves

Stafford

Burton
-on-Trent

SEVERN

Norbury
Junction

Gnosall

TRENT & MERSEY

Shrewsbury

Welshpool

Stretton

MONTGOMERY

Ironbridge

Wolverhampton

Autherley Junction
Aldersley Junction

BIRMINGHAM
& FAZELEY

COVENTRY

Newtown

STAFFS &
WORCS

Bratch

Birmingham

Bridgnorth

Swindon

Coventry

STOURBRIDGE

Edgbaston

Cookley

Kings
Norton

GRAND UNION

Bewdley

Kidderminster

WORCESTER &
BIRMINGHAM

Yardley
Wood

Stourport

Lapworth

SEVERN

Tardebigge

Wilmcote
Bearley

DROITWICH

Worcester

Stratford

Bidford

AVON

Welford

Fladbury

Pershore

Evesham

Upton on Severn

Eckington

Bredon

SEVERN

Tewkesbury

Cheltenham

The Weaver

The Weaver connects with the Manchester Ship Canal (see p. 102) at Weston Point, where there is a major dock complex, and for the first 13 miles of the navigation there is still a busy commercial traffic. The river itself is tidal, but vessels use a canalized section for the first four miles, after which the river is joined and followed to Pickering's Cut, one of the pleasantest reaches of the waterway. The cutting is narrow, tree-shaded and crossed by the tall Dutton viaduct. Dutton locks then lead back into the river and a gentle, wandering route with occasional glimpses of another waterway, the Trent & Mersey Canal, taking a high-level route along the valley rim (see p. 134). Natural river and artificial canal make their unlikely connection at the industrial centre of Anderton. The advantages of joining the two had long been obvious, but the problems of water for the locks, needed to cover a 50-feet change of level, proved insurmountable. Then, in 1875, the engineer Leader Williams found the answer – a lift to convey boats vertically between the two waterways. Originally, the Anderton Lift used two counter-balanced caissons, giant tubs of water into which boats could be floated. Later the system was changed to one in which each caisson was separately counter-balanced, as in a conventional lift, and moved by electric motor. Today, boats can still float out of the river into one of the caissons. Gates are closed behind them and up they go to be released at the top onto a short aqueduct leading into the Trent & Mersey.

The Weaver itself continues through the old salt town of Northwich and out into the lovely Vale Royal to Winsford. Here navigation ends at Winsford flash, an artificial lake created by subsidence from salt mining. It is now a popular sailing area.

A narrow boat being lowered on to the Weaver on the Anderton Lift.

The Shropshire Union

The name 'union' tells you that this is an amalgam of different canals: the Birmingham & Liverpool Junction, the Chester Canal and the Ellesmere Canal, together with several branches. The Ellesmere Canal is now known as the Llangollen, and the Shropshire Union is generally thought of as the main line from the Staffordshire & Worcestershire to Ellesmere Port, together with the Middlewich branch. Being an amalgam, its different parts have quite different characteristics.

The northern terminus, Ellesmere Port, was one of the great show pieces of the canal system until a large part of Telford's warehouse complex was burned down in 1970. It was unique as far as the canal system went, a major port development from which an important industrial town was to grow. Not everything was lost in the fire, however, and the surviving part is now home to an important collection of inland waterways boats, and some of the old dock machinery has been preserved. It is hard to imagine a better location for a canal museum, standing as it does between the narrow canal and the broad waters of the Mersey, and the establishment of the museum has done a great deal to encourage pleasure boaters to visit the area.

The first few miles of the canal take it across the wide plain of the Wirral, where the works of man dominate the works of nature. It is a measure of the importance of the canal that Ellesmere Port, which did not exist at all until the canal was built, should have grown into such an important industrial centre.

The next major stopping place could scarcely provide a greater contrast. This is the old walled city of Chester, and how splendidly a canal journey catches the different moods and different ages of the place. The first introduction comes with Tower Wharf and the connection with

The boat museum at Ellesmere Port and the first lock on the Shropshire Union.

The Shropshire Union

the Dee (see p. 112), reminders that Chester was once the most important port of the North West. Then the city walls themselves are reached, providing the energetic walker with a complete circuit of the city via the ramparts. Energy is also required on the canal to cope with the three-lock Northgate Staircase, after which the canal takes on the character of a moat, running in a rocky cutting round the walls.

From Chester to Nantwich is the oldest part of the Shropshire Union, the original Chester Canal. The chief distinguishing features are the broad locks, and some quirky buildings, such as the little round huts where the lock keepers could put their feet up for a few minutes' rest. Industry is now virtually left behind, in fact the nearest thing to industrial units to be met along the way are the old water-mills, for the Shropshire Union is very much a through route,

designed less to serve places along the way than to provide the quickest path between the Midlands and the Mersey. This, of course, suits today's holiday makers very well indeed, as the old canal makes its way through the broad pastures of the Cheshire plain, with views across to the distant hills. It is a canal of quiet pleasures, with few dramatic moments. There is, however, a fine variety of architecture – the old mill at Christleton, ruined Beeston Castle, perched on its high mound, and the handsome stable block built by the Shropshire Union Company beside the two-lock staircase at Bunbury.

At Barbridge, the ten-mile-long Middlewich Arm turns east to the Trent & Mersey (see p. 136), a very rural route, scarcely touching habitation, its high embankments providing wide views across the Weaver valley. A short way beyond, on the main line, is Hurleston

reservoir, providing the canal with water, and the entrance to the Llangollen Canal (see p. 112). Nantwich Basin then marks the end of the Chester Canal and the start of the Birmingham & Liverpool Junction. The canal, built under Telford's direction at the very end of the canal age, is a narrow canal which epitomizes the sophisticated engineering of the period. It is the 'cut and fill' canal *par excellence* – deep cuttings carving into the hills, high banks striding the valleys. This note of modernity is struck at once at Nantwich where the main road is crossed on a short cast-iron aqueduct. Telford used standard castings, which can be seen again on this canal and on the contemporary Macclesfield. Nantwich was, like the other 'wich' towns, founded on the salt trade, and much of it dates from the late sixteenth century when it was rebuilt after a fire. As much of Tudor Nantwich remains,

together with some excellent Regency additions, the walk into the town is well worth the effort.

The canal itself continues, following a straight line through farmland to Audlem. Locks are infrequent interruptions on this route, for when they do come they tend to be bunched close together in flights. This is the largest group, but what might look like hard work on a map, in practice turns out to be a pleasure, for the locks are beautifully maintained and as easy to work as any on the system. The start of the climb is marked by an attractive canal grouping of lock cottage and warehouses, the latter converted into pub and shops. The 15 Audlem locks are scarcely gone

Left The canal in its deep cutting beside the city walls of Chester.

Below Tyrley cutting and lock.

before the five Adderley locks appear, but again the attractive setting and ease of working make for pleasure not pain. One of the many tree-lined cuttings of the route leads on towards the market town of Market Drayton, an unpretentiously attractive spot. The canal now climbs again through one of the most beautiful flights of locks in the country, Tyrley locks, carved out of sandstone and shaded by a roof of trees.

Once the locks are past, the canal refuses to climb any further and dives through the hill in the deep, deep cutting at Woodseaves. As you go through, it is worth pausing to wonder at how such a cutting was made with nothing more powerful than the strong arms of the navvies. Now the pattern of the canal becomes established: first you meet the enclosed world of the deep cuttings, then you come out into the open to climb over the fields on a high embankment, for

Woodseaves Cutting is soon followed by the mighty Shebdon Bank. The alternation continues with Grub Street Cutting and Shelmore Bank leading to Gnosall and a brief underground excursion through the Cowley Tunnel, carved out of the bare rock.

After that the drama eases; cuttings are shallower, banks lower, though the scenery is no less pleasing. There is much to admire in the canal itself, such as the ornate Stretton aqueduct and even more ornate Avenue Bridge, decorated to satisfy a local landowner. But perhaps the most remarkable bridge of all is the last, remarkable not for its ornamentation, but for the simple elegance and absolute rightness of its lines. The junction bridge at Autherley carries the towpath of the Staffordshire & Worcestershire across the Shropshire Union: a memorable end to a memorable canal.

The Dee/The Llangollen Canal

The Dee

The Dee can be reached from the Shropshire Union Canal at Chester – but not with ease. A short cut and a lock lead down to the tidal river, but the river can be used only by giving prior notice and by arriving at the right time, for passage upstream depends on crossing the navigation weir. Inland waterway craft should keep clear of the lower tidal river, so timing is crucial as the weir can only be crossed at high spring tide. The water has to rise above the top of the weir to allow a gate to be opened which admits craft up to three feet draught onto the higher river. Once safely over, there are 12 pleasant miles of river to explore until progress is halted at Farndon Bridge.

There is a good deal of day boat traffic on the Dee in summer, particularly at Chester, which is left via a more or less straight stretch, a mile long and very popular with oarsmen. After that, the river follows a winding course across the plain, past pretty Eccleston to a remarkably handsome iron bridge, not dissimilar to the better known Waterloo Bridge at Betws-y-Coed. The far older Farndon Bridge once allowed trading vessels to pass through a navigation arch, but this is no more, and the boater is left with the option of mooring in Wales at one end of the bridge or in England at the other.

The Llangollen Canal

This is one of the best known and most popular canals in Britain, yet it was made famous by one spectacular feature and one short stretch that is really little more than a canal afterthought. It is easy to see how this has occurred, but it is rather a shame that over-emphasis of one part has tended to leave the rest undervalued. For if ever a canal could be said to show virtually every aspect of the engineer's craft, then the Llangollen is that canal. And this brings us to yet one more paradox. Ask most people to name the engineer responsible, and they will answer 'Telford'. And they would be wrong, for Telford was only called in when the work was already well under way, and then merely as assistant to the Llangollen's true begetter, William Jessop.

At Hurleston, the canal lifts straight up from the Shropshire Union via a flight of four locks, grouped conveniently together, after which the route heads south through the gentle farming country that accompanies so much of this canal. There follows a steady spattering of locks, but nothing too strenuous, and there are also a number of lift bridges. Happy murmurings of 'how quaint' and 'just like Van Gogh' disappear rapidly as crews save their breath for the effort of lifting. The second major group of locks comes at Grindley Brook with six of them, the last three run together as a staircase. It is a lovely spot, graced by an unusually elaborate, verandahed lock cottage. Beyond that is the entrance to the disused Whitchurch Arm, followed by an area that proved a major obstacle to the engineers, Whixall Moss. It is a botanist's delight but an engineer's nightmare, a vast bog which could only be crossed by the construction of a long embankment. A second disused arm, the Prees Branch, leads away, while the

Below Aerial view of the Pontcysyllte Aqueduct which spans the River Dee at a height of 120 feet.

Right One of the many lift bridges characteristic of the Llangollen.

The Llangollen Canal

main line clears the bog to head for a miniature Lake District. It wanders past the tree-shaded waters then through a short tunnel to emerge at Ellesmere. This is the town which gave the canal its original name – and gave a name to Ellesmere Port, but where the latter has grown and grown, the little market town has remained much as it was when the canal was new. The town centre is reached via a short arm opposite the rather odd, mock-Tudorish canal maintenance yard.

Beyond Ellesmere, the land erupts into a series of humps and bumps, which the canal threads by following a contour in the best Brindley tradition, twisting and turning to Frankton Junction and the start of the Montgomery (see p. 115). The next few miles are pleasantly uneventful, but the drama of the canal is about to begin. The route emerges high above the Ceiriog valley, hugging the hillside, lifted even higher above the land by an embankment. Then a sharp bend

brings the canal onto Chirk aqueduct that takes it high over the river. It would be a remarkable journey on any other canal, but here it is only a prelude to what lies ahead. The valley crossing over, the canal at once disappears into a deep, wooded cutting ending in a tunnel. There is one more short tunnel before the canal swings round to follow the Dee valley, which it is soon to cross. This was the barrier which gave most concern to the engineers. How should it be crossed? There were proposals for building locks down one side of the valley and up the other; various forms of aqueduct were suggested. Then the assistant, Telford, went off to work on the Shrewsbury Canal and came back with a plan for an aqueduct consisting of a light, cast-iron trough perched on high stone pillars. The plan was agreed, the Pontcysyllte was built, over 1000 feet long, its trough raised 120 feet above the waters of the Dee. Crossing it is quite unlike any other canal experience, for

the sides of the narrow trough are generally out of sight beneath the sides of the boat, so that one seems to be flying not boating.

Originally, the line continued straight on to Ruabon and the iron works that supplied the canal with trade. An arm was also constructed to join the Dee beyond Llangollen to provide a regular water supply. It was narrow but navigable, if only just. Today, it is this feeder channel that is used by pleasure boats, offering a superb end to the journey with a passage high up on the wooded hillside to Llangollen. How ironic that it is this tiny, almost insignificant feeder, scarcely used in working days, which has now become so important that it has given this magnificent canal its new name.

The approach to the Ellesmere Tunnel.

The Montgomery Canal

The Montgomery represents one of the major canal restoration projects currently under way. It is a curious upside down canal, starting at Frankton Junction, then going downhill to a point near Welshpool and then climbing up again to Newtown. Progress has already been considerable, though not without its bizarre aspects, with local authorities offering financial help with one hand, and passing plans for new roads that would effectively stop all navigation with the other. There are still many problems to be solved, including low bridges and dried up sections where the canal is all but invisible. The route is 35 miles long with 25 locks and a major aqueduct, so it is obvious that there is much to do if it is all to be reopened – and the different authorities are far from unanimous about whether or not it should be reopened throughout or only in part. Canal lovers have absolutely no doubt on that score, being firmly convinced that this route should again be opened to boats, enabling them to travel to the heart of the Welsh hills.

At the time of writing, seven miles in the middle of the canal have already been fully restored. Unfortunately, this is divided into two sections by a low bridge: five miles on one side, two on the other. It does, however, serve as an appetizing sample of the true flavour of the canal. The canal hugs a flank of the Severn valley, giving splendid views of the hills, while the town of Welshpool is just the sort of place where one would be happy to moor for a while, an attractive town with an added attraction in the shape of a preserved narrow gauge steam railway. Further north, a four-mile section which includes the Vyrnwy aqueduct has been restored, but it too has been closed off by a low bridge. It is also hoped that the completion of work on the locks at Frankton will mean that boats will again be turning off the Llangollen to cruise the Montgomery, if only for a tantalizingly short distance.

The restored Welsh Frankton Lock takes boats from the Llangollen on to the Montgomery Canal.

The Severn

The river has shrunk, at least in terms of navigation, to a mere fraction of what it was even as recently as a century ago. Then trading vessels could pass far up river, even right through into Wales. Today, for most practical purposes, navigation stops at Stourport, though small craft can struggle on as far as Bewdley. The sad thing is that it is precisely those upper levels that have been lost to navigation which have the most to offer. One has only to contemplate the possibility, for example, of being able to boat down the Ironbridge Gorge to long for a return of the old days – and now there is a glimmer of hope that those days might again return. 1982 saw the publication of a plan for the restoration of navigation as high as Ironbridge. In the meantime, one is left with a big, wide river, too wide perhaps to give that feeling of intimacy with the landscape that is such an important part of the special charm of the waterways. Nevertheless, this is a river that is much used, if not so much for its own sake then as a connecting link between other, more attractive routes. It is all a sad falling off from the old river which was the mightiest and busiest trading route in Britain.

Bewdley, for those shallow draught vessels which can make it this far, is a fascinating spot which, in its day, was a thriving inland port. All that, however, is well in the past, for trade began to slip away following the construction of the Staffordshire & Worcestershire Canal (see p. 120). This joins the river lower down, and it was at that junction that Stourport grew from a solitary inn to become a port to rival Bewdley. The area round the docks still retains all the character of the Georgian town. Not that this is the main impression gained by the river traveller, who is more likely to be aware of the adjoining power station, followed by the first of the big, manned locks.

As with so many rivers, the general rule about the scenery – the higher up river the better – applies to the Severn. On the first part of the journey, south from Stourport, the river is bordered by wooded hills, which keep it company until Worcester is reached. The river provides magnificent views of the cathedral, beyond which is the entrance to the Worcester & Birmingham Canal (see p. 119). Below this point, the river scenery suffers from that common complaint of high banks which cut off most of the view, so that interest becomes concentrated on the towns met along the way. Upton-upon-Severn is quite the most attractive place to stop for a while, while at Tewkesbury boats can turn off into the Avon (see p. 117). A separate licence is required for the Avon, but it is possible to travel as far as Healing's Mill for free, where you can moor and walk the rest. The rest of the river is now tidal, and is closed to navigation at Gloucester. Here vessels must turn into the lock cutting for Gloucester docks and the start of the Gloucester & Sharpness Canal (see p. 144).

Below The Severn running past Worcester Cathedral.

The Avon

Those who turn off the Severn into the Avon generally experience an immediate uplift of the spirits, for while the lower Severn may offer a quick way of getting from A to B it is undeniably dull. The Avon is far slower, but also far more attractive: it is rather as if one were turning off a motorway and into a quiet country lane. The Avon is one of the restoration movement's success stories. At present it has two parts, the Lower Avon to Evesham and the Upper to Stratford, and there are hopes that the success story will be continued with the restoration of the Higher Avon to Warwick.

The entrance to the river is marked by Healing's Mill, after which a lock leads into Tewkesbury. This particular lock is manned, but most on the river are strictly do-it-yourself. The town itself is an ancient foundation, centred on the great abbey, and the river is crossed by a bridge of almost equal antiquity, King John's Bridge. It is the first of many old multi-arched bridges on the river which must be negotiated with care. Once safely through the bridge, Tewkesbury is soon left astern and the river comes into its own. It is, to say the least, a meandering river: the well co-ordinated crow could make a 24-mile flight from Tewkesbury to Stratford; the river traveller covers 44 miles. Unlike the Severn, there are no high banks to impede the view, while the twists and turns ensure a constantly changing scene – and require an alert steerer. Bredon Hill, topped by its Iron Age fort, dominates the early part of the scenery, while the delightful village of Bredon offers good moorings. Sadly, for such a beautiful river, good moorings are not always so easy to come by, with 'Keep Off' notices sprouting like weeds along the banks. Locks can also present a few tricky problems, with awkward approaches.

Eckington has two bridges, separated by centuries, yet both are splendid examples of stylish use of materials: a railway bridge of iron on stone piers, and the medieval sandstone road bridge. The river now traces a gigantic S-bend on its way to Pershore, another fine town of ancient buildings mixed with Georgian and modern, grain mill and orchards defining the trade of the town. Orchards proliferate in this area round Evesham, but unlike the main fruit growing area of the Vale this is still very hilly country. At Fladbury there is an item of considerable historical interest, the remains of

Fladbury water-mill and ferry.

the old flash lock. Evesham, another quietly attractive town, has an item of interest of more recent date. The lock cottage is built on an unusual A-frame design, but in spite of its modernity is very much in keeping with its surroundings.

The Upper Avon is as attractive – and as meandering – as the Lower, and contains some of the more awkward lock problems. Robert Aickman Lock, named after the Inland Waterways pioneer, stands at right angles to the river and is very difficult to use. All the locks on the Upper Avon are new, for when the navigation resumed in 1970 the river had been unused for a century. Perhaps one should not worry too much about any shortcomings and simply be thankful the river can be used at all. The upper river is again like the lower in that it too offers lovely scenery, delightful towns such as Bidford and Welford, and still more fine bridges. The last two bridges at Stratford are particularly interesting; the first originally carried a horse-drawn tramway and the second is the old toll bridge in the town centre. Stratford is, of course, world famous for its best known son, Shakespeare, and there is surely no better way to get here than by water, mooring up under the shadow of the Memorial Theatre. Here, for the present, navigation ends, but one's journey need not for this is also the starting point for the Stratford Canal.

The Stratford-upon-Avon Canal

The canal is not just another restoration success, but *the* restoration success, for the southern Stratford was the first waterway to be restored to navigation by volunteer efforts. It was reopened in 1964 after years of lying derelict, since when it has proved immensely popular. It has also provided a lesson for the volunteer movement. It is not enough simply to restore a canal: it must be maintained as well. Two decades of use have demonstrated all too clearly the problems and expenses of keeping a canal going once the initial euphoria of the reopening has passed. The lower section of the canal came under the ownership of the National Trust, while the upper section remained with B.W.B. This is not quite the arbitrary division that it might appear since the upper section remained viable as a link between Birmingham and the Grand Union, while the other half atrophied, leading nowhere but to the then unnavigable Avon. The division makes little difference to the boater, who simply accepts the Stratford as a particularly attractive and inviting waterway.

The basin at Stratford is very much at the centre of the Bard's town, but once that has been left behind a new workaday Stratford appears. The workaday canal soon follows in the shape of the Wilmcote locks, 11 of them leading up to Wilmcote itself and almost the last of the Shakespearian reminders on the canal, Mary Arden's cottage. The canal now has the rural character which it retains throughout most of its length. It is difficult to say which provides the most interest on the route, the Warwickshire countryside or the canal structures themselves. There is a lot to be said for the latter: unique barrel-vaulted lock cottages, iron bridges split down the centre to allow tow ropes to pass through, and aqueducts, especially Bearley – an iron trough which runs for nearly 500 feet across the Alne valley.

At Lapworth the restored section meets the B.W.B. section at a point where the Stratford Canal is joined to the Grand Union (see p. 51) halfway up the Lapworth flight, which completes the long climb up to the level of the Birmingham plateau. Although the city is quite near, it makes little impression on the canal until Yardley Wood. Here there is a short tunnel and a last reminder of Shakespeare, whose bust stands in a niche above the portals. The Stratford Canal reaches the Worcester & Birmingham at King's Norton.

Below Bearley Aqueduct.

The Worcester & Birmingham Canal

This is a canal with a somewhat fearsome reputation, largely earned by being able to claim the longest flight of locks in Britain. As a consequence, many boaters fight shy of it, which is a shame because it is an attractive waterway, offering one of the pleasantest and most interesting routes into Birmingham. Although there are many locks, they prove to be less formidable in practice than they might seem in theory.

The canal has a fascinating start at Diglis Basin in the centre of Worcester, joined to the river by two broad locks. As so often on the canals, the waterway provides a unique perspective on a well known place. The cathedral and the elegant city are still plainly visible, but so too is the other city, the trading and commercial centre, home of Worcester porcelain. Old Worcester appears at King's Head Lock, in the lovely form of the Commandery, a restored fifteenth-century hospital. After that the canal returns to the industrial suburbs but once these are left behind the route takes on the rural aspect that will remain with it through to the outskirts of Birmingham. The steady climb out of the Severn valley continues with 16 locks in the first half-dozen miles. The M5 clattering overhead marks the start of one of the few rest periods of over five lock-free miles in which to enjoy the placid Worcestershire countryside, briefly abandoned for the dark of Dunhampstead Tunnel. The derelict Droitwich Canal, which it is hoped one day will be restored, appears on one side of the canal while the far older route, the ancient track known as the Salt Way, appears on the other. Soon the locks start again, with the Astwood and Stoke flights as preludes to Tardebigge. Fortunately for the fainthearted, the flight follows a curving path so that one is not faced by the sight of all 30 locks grouped together. The pub at the bottom of the flight does a roaring trade between those stoking up for their labours and those taking their reward for having come down. Yet how easily these locks seem to go, helped by the pleasant surroundings, though there is no denying that the sight of the reservoir and pumping station at the top is always welcome.

Having reached the top, crews can relax secure in the knowledge that their lock working is over, for it is now level all the way through to Birmingham, thanks to two tunnels, short Tardebigge and 2726-yard-long King's Norton, which

between them cope with the remainder of the hills. King's Norton also marks the approach of Birmingham and what a fascinating approach it is, alternating the sweet airs of Bournville and the chocolate factory with leafy cuttings such as Edgbaston. Then, quite suddenly it seems, one has arrived at the centre of the city.

Above The top lock at Tardebigge, the longest lock flight in Britain.

Below Stoke Works.

The Staffordshire & Worcestershire Canal

This is very much a Brindley canal, built to join the Severn to the Trent & Mersey Canal as part of a grander scheme, known as the Cross, which linked the four major rivers of England – Severn, Trent, Mersey and Thames. It was here that the standards were set for the whole Midland system, for it was on this canal that the first narrow locks were built. It is not necessary, however, to put the canal into any sort of historical perspective in order to succumb to its charms.

The junction at Stourport (see p. 116) between the Severn and the canal grew to such importance precisely because of Brindley's decision to opt for the narrow canal. It became a trans-shipment point between the river barges, the sailing trows of the Severn, and the narrow boats. It is a perfect Georgian introduction to a Georgian canal, and the same qualities of fine proportion and fitness for the job mark both the terminus buildings and the surrounding area. It seems that peaceful elegance might prove the hallmark of the canal, but then on the outskirts of Kidderminster that all changes. Sandstone cliffs rear up above the waterway, and they are to remain with the canal for many miles to come. The passage through the town itself was once equally dramatic, but wholesale demolition of the older industrial buildings has reduced it to comparatively dull ordinariness. Once through the town, the canal is everything you could wish for from the authorship of James Brindley. It twists and wriggles under the ever-present shadow of the red sandstone, which it pierces in a tunnel under the village of Cookley, where the sandstone has also been carved away to provide lockside stabling. Locks are evenly spaced and each seems more delightful than the last, not a false note being struck in this magnificent passage. There is one junction offering a short cut to Birmingham via the Stourbridge

Above The canal creeping below the sandstone cliffs at Falling Sands Lock.

Right The Bratch, with its octagonal toll house by the top lock.

Canal (see p. 126) but few are tempted to forsake these delectable wanderings.

The scenery has settled down to normality by the time Swindon is reached but the canal itself more than compensates by its own best known feature, the Bratch. Three locks stand together, separated by only a few inches of water. It is an extraordinary system, with water being stored in ponds off to one side. Why Brindley did not run the whole lot together as a staircase is a mystery, but canal travellers should be the last to complain about strange quirks and idiosyncrasies, particularly when the whole flight is crowned by a gently curving bridge and octagonal toll house. The next few miles would be considered splendid anywhere else, but after what has gone before can seem a mild anti-climax, an uneventful cruise to the edge of Wolverhampton.

Two junctions appear close together, one with the Birmingham Canal (see p. 124) the second with the Shropshire Union (see p. 110) and these are followed by a very odd little section where the canal is cut through solid rock. This obviously proved hard work for the builders, for the channel is only wide enough to allow one-way passage. The canal here runs unusually straight for Brindley but that changes at Coven, where it practically goes into convulsions. The countryside epitomizes the rural Midlands, a land of farms and villages, fields and copses, a quiet land that would be quieter still were it not for occasional incursions by the M6. But that is a minor irritation, and the canal reaches a grand conclusion opening out into Tixall Broad with a distant view of the ornate Tixall gatehouse. Even that is not quite the end of the story for the junction with the Trent & Mersey (see p. 136) at Great Haywood, near Stafford, is crossed by a supremely elegant bridge.

The East Midlands

This is an area of dramatic contrasts. It contains the Trent & Mersey Canal, the first major trunk route to be built in Britain, a fascinating waterway which combines attractive scenery with old industrial centres. There are the rural delights of the Oxford, and the impressive engineering of the Leicester Arm of the Grand Union. Then, at the heart of the region, stands Birmingham, built on a plateau whose sides the canals clamber up in all directions to reach the complex labyrinth of the Birmingham Canal Navigations. Even the smaller canals that complete the area are as different one from the other as can be imagined. Those who cannot find something to suit their tastes in this region might just as well turn away from the canals for ever. Not surprisingly, some find certain parts far more appealing than others, but those who find themselves equally intrigued by everything in the region can reasonably claim membership of that select body known as the True Enthusiasts.

The Birmingham Canal Navigations

The Birmingham & Fazeley Canal

The Coventry Canal

The Ashby Canal

The Oxford Canal

The Trent & Mersey Canal

The Caldon Canal

The Grand Union, Leicester Section

The Erewash

The Cromford Canal

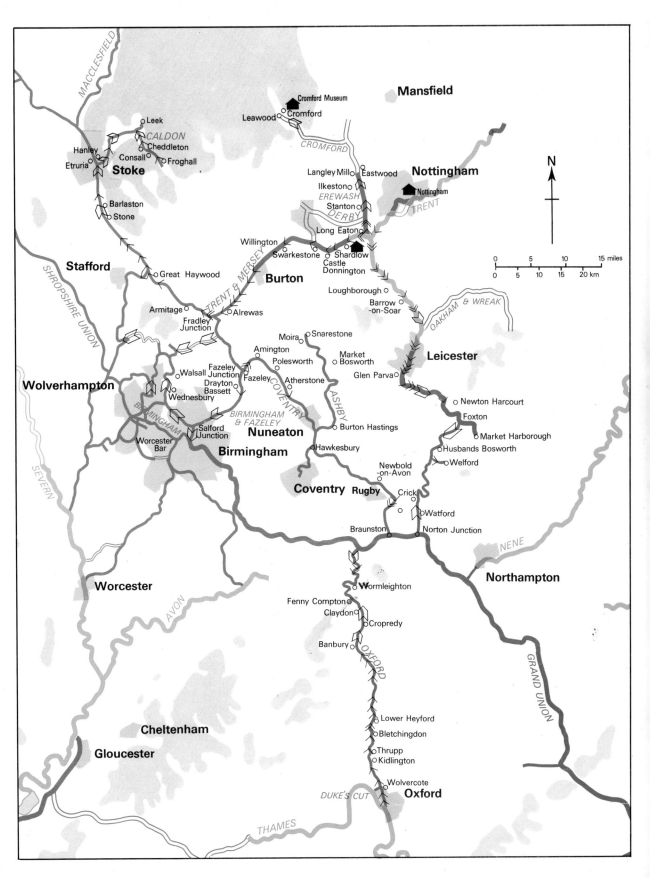

Macclesfield

Leek
CALDON
Cheddleton
Hanley
Etruria
Consall
Froghall
Stoke

Barlaston
Stone

Stafford

SHROPSHIRE UNION

Wolverhampton

Walsall
Wednesbury

Worcester
Bar

SEVERN

Worcester

Gloucester

Cheltenham

AVON

Cromford Museum
Leawood
Cromford

CROMFORD

Mansfield

Nottingham

Langley Mill
Eastwood
Ilkeston
EREWASH
Stanton
DERBY
Long Eaton

TRENT

Great Haywood

Armitage
Fradley
Junction
Alrewas

Willington
Swarkestone
Shardlow
Castle
Donnington

Moira
Snarestone

Amington
Polesworth
Fazeley
Junction
Fazeley
Drayton
Bassett
Atherstone

COVENTRY

ASHBY

Loughborough
Barrow
-on-Soar

OAKHAM & WREAK

Market
Bosworth
Glen Parva

Leicester

Newton Harcourt

Foxton
Market Harborough

BIRMINGHAM
& FAZELEY

Salford
Junction

Nuneaton

Birmingham

Burton Hastings

Hawkesbury

Coventry   Rugby

Newbold
-on-Avon

Husbands Bosworth
Welford

Crick

Braunston
Watford
Norton Junction

NENE

Northampton

Worcester

GRAND UNION

Wormleighton

Fenny Compton
Claydon
Cropredy

Banbury

OXFORD

Lower Heyford
Bletchingdon
Thrupp
Kidlington
Wolvercote

DUKE'S CUT   Oxford

THAMES

N

0   5   10   15 miles
0   5   10   15
0   5   10   15   20 km

The Birmingham Canal Navigations

The engine house rises high above the Dudley No. 2 Canal at Windmill End.

The Birmingham Canal Navigations, commonly referred to as the B.C.N., is a complex system that spreads across the whole of the Birmingham plateau and down its flanks. Some will always wish to hurry through, averting their eyes from the sometimes grim, and almost invariably grimy, evidence of the industrial base of this country's economic life. A trip on the B.C.N. provides a new insight into how the Black Country got its name, for the canal water itself is frequently the colour of blue-black ink and the consistency of watery soup. But Birmingham is the canal capital of Britain, a city which grew with and around its canals – a city which could scarcely have grown without them. For those whose interests go beyond the merely scenic, who see their boat trip as something more than just another way to enjoy the scenery, the B.C.N. can offer something uniquely fascinating. The vital part that canals played in establishing Britain as the world's first industrial nation can never be seen more

clearly than it is here. No one would call the area pretty, though some parts are, but those who have spent any time on the B.C.N. are apt to find themselves returning time and again for fresh explorations.

The B.C.N. is a complex in every sense, of old canals and new canals, branches and loops, but through the centre of it all runs the main line. Even that is not as simple as it might seem, for there are actually two main lines, the original Birmingham Canal, designed by Brindley with his customary whirls and squiggles, and the new, improved version built by Telford. The new cuts right through the bends of the old, leaving them as loops, rarely used backwaters. For many, the new main line is all that they see, providing the through route from Birmingham to Wolverhampton. It starts officially at Worcester Bar, the junction with the Worcester & Birmingham Canal (see p. 119) and at once something of the special nature of the B.C.N. appears, in the shape of Gas

Street Basin. Until recently this area was totally enclosed, a private canal world shut away behind the old wharf buildings, scarcely visible from the city streets. Sadly, demolition has destroyed much of that special atmosphere, but not all of it, and Gas Street is still home to many narrow boats. A short tunnel under the main road brings the busy Farmer's Bridge Junction, the way marked by a signpost set on an odd little traffic island which for once really is an island. To the right is an area that has been developed but keeps the familiar canal buildings, lock cottage, toll house and pub, standing at the top of the Birmingham & Fazeley Canal (see p. 128). The new main line carries straight on, but the old Brindley line drifts off to the left in the Oozells Street Loop, where there is a hire base and moorings,

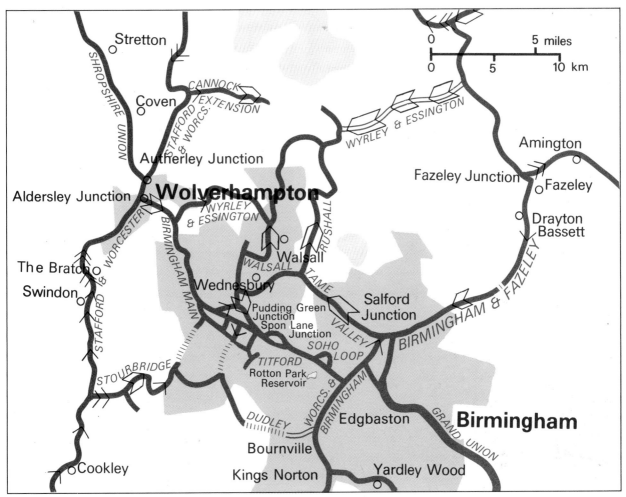

before returning to the new line. This pattern of main line striding resolutely forward while the old goes its own devious way is followed throughout. The next pair of loops are Icknield Port, running below the bank of Rotton Park reservoir, and Soho, which goes past the site of the Soho works, the famous factory established by the steam engine pioneers, Boulton and Watt.

The main line keeps straight by means of an impressively deep cutting, while the old line climbs to a higher level through three locks. The difference between the two is most striking: the old being crossed by the familiar hump-backed brick bridges, while the bridges across the new are monumental, culminating in the great cast-iron span of Galton Bridge. A branch of the old line, the Engine Arm, also crosses the new line on an ornate iron aqueduct full of Gothic arches and decorative swirls. Beyond that is a remarkable complex. The old line branches, the main part crossing the new on the Steward aque-duct, while a branch joins the new through the Spon Lane locks. To add to the drama, the M6 swoops overhead, supported on vast pillars that stand in the middle of the canal. Now the Telford line heads straight for its destination through a landscape that still carries the scars of industrial exploitation, the route parallel to the main line railway. Junctions appear at regular intervals, starting with the splendidly named Pudding Green and the Walsall Canal. The old canal follows a roughly parallel course, before the two again merge at Factory Junction, only to part once more at the Wednesbury Oak Loop. A word of warning here for those who explore the old loops: be prepared for rubbish in the water. It was on this particular branch that the author collected a tangle of oil cloth and wire round the propellor which could be removed only by oxy-acetylene burner!

Wolverhampton stands at the edge of the plateau, and the canal winds through its industrial centre before plunging down through a flight of 21 locks. The top is a purely industrial landscape of engineering works and foundries, with the aromas of the nearby brewery drifting across the waters. The bottom of the flight is a complete contrast, open country and the junction with the Staffordshire & Worcestershire (see p. 120).

This then is the main line, but it forms only a fraction of the whole B.C.N. network, which offers an intriguing variety of routes, and you can be fairly certain of not being bothered by great crowds of fellow boaters. There are short diversions, such as that along the Titford Canal which survives mainly as a feeder, but which takes you past the hugely impressive Langley Maltings. There are also main routes leading off south to other parts of the canal system, such as the two Dudley Canals though, at the time of writing, progress down these is stopped by tunnel closures. The new tunnel is the long, wide Netherton Tunnel, running parallel to the original Dudley Tunnel. The old canal takes

The Birmingham Canal Navigations

you to the Black Country Museum, built around the canal basin at the northern end of the tunnel, and it is well worth visiting. So too is Dudley Tunnel, which alternates low, cramped passages with vast underground caverns. But, and it is a very important but, only quite low boats can pass through and even then, as there is no ventilation, engines must not be used. If you have a small boat and fancy legging (pushing the boat through by walking your feet against the tunnel walls), then fine: if not, then do it the easy way and take a ride on the special electrically-powered trip boat. At the far end, the scene is surprisingly rural as the Park Head locks lead down past the old pumping station, but industry is soon back in a spectacular fashion, as the canal swoops down to the factories through the eight Delph locks to Stourbridge and the Stourbridge Canal. This again has some surprisingly open sections and, as you descend the 16 locks, you pass one of the unique industrial monuments of the area, an eighteenth-century glass cone or furnace, before the canal joins up with the Staffordshire & Worcestershire.

The northern network is far more extensive, with a group of canals running round in an enormous loop. The first part is formed by the Wyrley & Essington, a true B.C.N. canal, very wayward in line, alternating busy industrial scenes with open sections that you simply would not believe could be

Above The eighteenth-century glass cone beside the Stourbridge Canal.

Right Gas Street Basin, home to many narrow boats.

found in this area. It begins at the top of Wolverhampton locks and you get the mixture thrown at you right away: industry to start with, the M6 zooms up alongside and then all of a sudden you find a nature trail. After that, just to keep you on your toes, there is a vicious hairpin, followed by a choice of routes. You can turn back to the main line down the Walsall Canal or take the more enticing option and carry on with the Wyrley & Essington. Off it curls again,

though there is a dead straight arm that can be followed up to a traditional canal boatyard, the Cannock Extension. The Wyrley, however, has nothing to do with straight lines and it swings again, almost completing a circle, to reach Daw End and the Rushall Canal. At Rushall Junction, you can take the Tame Valley Canal back towards the Walsall Canal or onwards to a quite remarkable end. The Tame Valley is a modern canal of straight lines, ending at Salford Junction,

the most amazing spot on the whole B.C.N. network. There is a four-way canal junction, with a river underneath, and striding over everything is the concrete tangle of Spaghetti Junction. The circuit is nearly over, the way back up to Birmingham being up the Birmingham & Fazeley Canal. This is not the end of the B.C.N., however, for there remains a host of varied and intriguing arms and branches waiting for the enthusiastic explorer.

The Birmingham & Fazeley Canal

The route begins at Farmer's Bridge Junction (see p. 124) and at once begins dropping down through locks, between old factories and warehouses which once saw the canal as a major life line. Their successor, the modern tower block, simply squats on top of the canal and tries to pretend it is not there. The locks run past the Science and Industry Museum, which turns an equally disinterested face to the waterway on which the industry it celebrates was built. There is a brief respite and then the 11 Aston locks lead the canal down to Salford Junction (see p. 127). This is a turning point on the canal, for as it comes out from the shadow of the motorway, it begins to lose that very hemmed-in feeling that characterized the upper section. There are still factories, but more modern, built well after the canal age so paying little heed to the waterway; a noble exception being the Cincinnati Works where lawns come down to the water.

Soon even the modern factories are left behind, as the canal heads north through a peaceful landscape, dropping steadily down to the Tame valley. At Drayton Bassett there is a zoo, and a bizarre footbridge with little castellated towers. At the very end, at Fazeley, industry returns in the somewhat surprising form of cotton mills, the oldest of which was founded by Robert Peel in 1790. Here too is the junction with the Coventry Canal.

The canal emerging from under a modern office block on the Farmer's Bridge flight of locks.

The Coventry Canal

This is another Brindley canal, built to link Coventry to the Trent & Mersey Canal with a connection to the Oxford to open the way to the south. It offers a pleasant route, but shows few of the extravagant curves that one might expect from a canal of this period. It does, however, have a splendid beginning at the old basin in the city centre. The first five and a half miles never seem to receive the attention they deserve, many boats simply passing on from the Coventry to the Oxford Canal, the line down to Coventry being regarded as a dead end of no interest. How wrong they are. It is an urban route certainly, but one full of interest. The canal passes such places as Cash's where the factory runs literally over the workers' houses in the form of the Top Shops, and there are reminders of an industrial life older than that in the eighteenth-century weavers'

and knitters' cottages.

The junction with the Oxford Canal (see p. 131) at Hawkesbury is a justifiably famous canal spot, with a low arched cast-iron bridge, old boaters' pub, canal cottages and the engine house where the Newcomen steam engine once worked, supplying the canal with water. The engine has been preserved in its own museum at Dartmouth. The industrial theme continues as the canal runs through a land bearing the unmistakable marks of coal mining, past the entrance to the Ashby Canal to a somewhat dull passage through Nuneaton. Beyond that is the functional and attractive Hartshill Maintenance Yard, soon followed by the 11 Atherstone locks, and more mining communities. Even when the mine has gone, the mining village is unmistakable; there is something unique in the long, straggling terraces of a

Hawkesbury Junction, also known as Sutton Stop, is a busy canal centre.

village such as Amington which absolutely proclaims its identity. It is not all mining along the way: there is a slightly glum Tudor manor and the remains of an abbey at Polesworth, but these seem little more than interruptions to the general scene.

A second flight of locks leads to an aqueduct across the Tame and Fazeley Junction. The final miles are through rich, undulating countryside which lasts until a deserted airfield announces the end of the line. Fradley Junction, where Coventry meets the Trent & Mersey (see p. 134), is an attractive group that is almost a match for Hawkesbury.

The Ashby Canal

The Ashby offers a lovely, gentle introduction to the world of canals, quite enough for a pleasant weekend's pottering and, once you have passed the stop lock at the junction with the Coventry Canal, not a lock to be seen. The character of the canal is established at once, and it is a character it retains throughout – tranquil, keeping shy of towns along the way. It can sound slightly dull, but turns out to be quite the opposite.

The first few miles are untypical, for there is a deep, wooded cutting near Burton Hastings, but once that is past the Ashby begins to snake off round low hills. It never quite manages to reach the towns along the way, just touches gently at their outer fringes. The towns are, however, worth the short walk from the canal. So too is the battle site at Bosworth Field – where Richard III offered his kingdom for a horse – and which now has a special interpretation centre. Market Bosworth itself is a pleasant market town, again some way from the canal, which can boast a brewing oddity, for the Red Lion is the one and only tied house owned by the local Hoskins brewery. At Shackerstone, the canal runs past the station of the Market Bosworth Railway, a preserved steam line which has a wonderfully higgledy-piggledy museum in the old waiting-room.

There are just three miles of quiet country before the canal pops under the village of Snarestone in a short tunnel to come to an abrupt end. Other sections can be walked, and at Moira there is a magnificent stone blast furnace built against the canal bank – which, if nothing else, does at least go some way towards explaining why this tranquil rural waterway was ever built in the first place.

Below The rural solitude that typifies the Ashby Canal.

The Oxford Canal

The Oxford is one of the country's most popular canals, and in summer it can suffer a good deal from overcrowding. Those who would rather avoid the crowds should travel out of season, but whenever you choose to travel this is certainly not a canal to be missed. Or perhaps one should say, these are not canals to be missed, for the Oxford divides between its southern and northern sections, and the character of the two halves could scarcely be more different. In fact, unless you know something of the history of the route, it can be quite bewildering.

When the Oxford was first laid out by James Brindley, it followed precisely the sort of wavering line that one would

expect, and so it would have remained had it not been for the arrival of the Grand Junction Canal at the end of the eighteenth century. This joined the Oxford at Braunston, and boats made extensive use of the northern section. Traffic built up, and the old wanderer proved less and less adequate, so at the end of the 1820s a new northern route was built which followed a straight line. And, as at Birmingham, the new line sliced up the old, leaving the original Brindley Canal as a series of side loops. The southern end was left alone, and remains the contour canal *par excellence.*

The canal's start at Hawkesbury (see p. 129) is another innovation, for origin-

Above The Oxford Canal meanders through the Cherwell Valley.

ally the Coventry and Oxford Companies were unable to agree on where to join, so the two canals ran side by side for miles, until reason at last prevailed. This is essentially a rural canal, starting off among the swelling, rolling fields of Warwickshire, a land of rich red soil and rich red brick houses, where little disturbs the peace. There are intrusions here – the M6 dashes across at one point – but they seem no more than minor incidents on the peaceful journey. From time to time, little iron bridges, bearing

The Oxford Canal

the announcement that they were cast at Horseley Iron Works appear, crossing weed-clogged branches. These mark the entrances to the old Brindley bends, and if you follow the old lines on foot you come across all kinds of strange little reminders of that route – wharves with no water, hump-backed bridges in the middle of ploughed fields. One of the most interesting diversions is at Newbold-on-Avon. The new canal passes through a short tunnel, while the old canal tunnel, on a quite different alignment, can be seen by the church.

The canal passes the edge of Rugby on an embankment and then reaches Hillmorton locks beside the canal maintenance yard. At Braunston, the Oxford and the Grand Union meet at what was, in its day, an important canal settlement. It remains one of the few places where working narrow boats may still be seen. The Oxford and Grand Union share a route for five miles to Napton, where the latter continues on to Birmingham (see p. 51) and the Oxford turns away to its southern section. This is the part that pulls the crowds, for it seems to epitomize all that is best on the rural canal. At the top of Napton-on-the-Hill stands the village with its twin emblems of the old country way of life – the ancient church tower and the windmill. Down below, the canal that has been restricted to straightness for a long time, shakes itself out into sinuous lines. Bridges of mellow red brick cross the route as it heads up the long straggle of Napton locks to its summit level. If ever there was a canal that seemed determined to take the longest distance between two points, this is it. It all reaches a climax at the Wormleighton bend, where you pass one side of a house on the hill and then, about a quarter of an hour later, arrive back again at the other side. Yet it is all so splendid that no one would ever begrudge the time spent on those extra miles. There is a surprise awaiting, however, at Fenny Compton, where the route suddenly goes dead straight in a deep cutting. The explanation is simple: this was originally a shallow tunnel, and then the top was lifted off.

The climb down from the summit begins at Claydon, and soon the first of the villages is reached by canal. Cropredy is typical of this part of Oxfordshire: thatched houses, built of rich, glowing ironstone, so picturesque they can seem unreal. The canal has now reached the Cherwell valley which it will

follow almost to Oxford. The one large town along the way is announced with a flurry of the simple lift bridges which are typical of the Oxford and a modern industrial estate which is not. Banbury itself, with its nursery-rhyme cross, is attractive, and although only a few of the old mills that once lined the canal have survived, the canal journey is not short of atmosphere. If it was notable for

nothing else, it would be for Tooley's yard, where narrow boats have been built and repaired ever since the canal was built.

The route to the south is now characterized by a string of little villages and old water-mills on the Cherwell. There is a sudden noisy intrusion at the Upper Heyford airbase, but Lower Heyford and beautiful Rousham Park are waiting

Above The canal in Cropredy, one of the most attractive villages along the route.

Right The elegant curves of one of the Horseley Iron Works bridges than span the old line of the Oxford Canal.

up ahead by way of compensation. Bletchingdon is signposted by the tall cement works chimney and here canal and river meet, boats travelling briefly on the Cherwell before they leave it again at the diamond-shaped Shipton Weir Lock. Thrupp, with its delightful canalside settlement, marks the parting between river and canal, and Kidlington is passed by as Oxford draws near. A short branch, Duke's Cut, leads down to the Thames, while the main line goes on past Wolvercote Green to the outskirts of Oxford. The city is famous for modern car manufacture as well as the university: the canal mostly sees the former. It ends, however, with the latter where Isis Lock leads down to the Thames and the canal finishes by the grounds of Worcester College. Once it continued on into a major wharf complex, but all that has vanished under car parks and Nuffield College. Nevertheless, the canal does take you to the city centre, and a walk up by Nuffield will bring you out by the handsome canal offices, as attractive as the canal they served. The canal is an agreeable and salutory reminder that the colleges are not the only beauties of Oxford.

The Trent & Mersey Canal

This was the great undertaking of the early canal age. It started with a tough political battle, led by the potter Josiah Wedgwood, to get the canal started, and this was followed by a sterner battle to get the canal built. Brindley was the man in charge, but he died before it was completed. Looking at the canal today, it seems a somewhat gentle affair with none of the obvious problems faced by later engineers who pushed their routes through the Pennine hills or across the Welsh valleys. But Brindley had no precedents to follow in Britain, for nothing on this scale had ever been attempted – a canal that was to stretch for nearly 100 miles, to link great rivers on opposite sides of the country. Seen in the perspective of history it is indeed a mighty undertaking, but seen in terms of today's pleasure boaters, it is not the scale of the enterprise that impresses, so much as the steady accumulation of small pleasures. The Trent & Mersey is a canal to be savoured as much for its mixture of the simple, but so satisfying, structures met along the way – locks, bridges, cottages – as for the scenery. It also offers a fascinating glimpse into the industrial past.

Starting at the junction with the Trent (see p. 77), one is immediately presented with precisely those pleasures, deriving directly from the canal, with which the route abounds. The town of Shardlow grew up around the offices and warehouses of the interchange port, where goods were exchanged between big river craft and canal narrow boats. It is a Georgian town in which the purely commercial buildings display the same qualities of good proportion and good taste as the houses. The former Trent Mill is a fine example, built over an arm of the canal to enable boats to float under the arch to load and unload. It now houses a canal exhibition. The adjoining lock comes as something of a surprise, since this is thought of as a narrow canal, and this is a wide lock. Such wide locks, however, only continue as far as Burton-on-Trent. The canal now leaves Shardlow to follow the lush, green Trent valley, with the inevitable accompaniment of power stations at Castle Donnington and Willington. The railway follows a similar, but less tortuous, line alongside. At Swarkestone, the entrance to the derelict Derby Canal is marked by a cluster of buildings, warehouses, stables and toll house.

The first town of any size is Burton-on-Trent, marked by the tall towers of the numerous breweries, though if the wind is in the right direction, you smell the town before you see it. The Bass Museum in the town gives due credit to the importance of the canal in the development of the area. Dallow Lane Lock is the first of the narrow locks and soon the canal enters one of its most attractive reaches. Tatenhill Lock, for example, shows all the features that one looks for on the early canals: a tiny bridge across the tail of the lock, the black and white balance beams and the neat little lock cottage add up to a perfect canal scene. There is a brief eruption of noise as the A38 appears alongside the canal, but they soon part again after which the canal runs into the Trent to pass through water meadows to Alrewas, with the ancient church of Wychnor as a focal point. To travel this way is to step into an animated Constable painting – though the steerer must temper such romantic notions with more prosaic thoughts to avoid the weir at the start of the river section. Beyond Alrewas a straight run leads to Fradley and the junction with the Coventry Canal (see p. 129).

The canal which has been heading south west now turns north, still following the Trent but looking forwards to the Mersey. It runs through heathland towards Armitage, and the first example of the industry the canal was to serve so well, ceramics. This is not exactly the home of delicate tea services, as the gleaming white loos piled high outside the factory testify. The working world stays for a while with colliery and power station before the crossing of the Trent on a low, somewhat cumbersome aqueduct marks the arrival of another very attractive open section. The Trent valley gradually closes in as the Trent & Mersey reaches Great Haywood and the junction with the Staffordshire & Worcestershire (see p. 121). The wide tracts of Cannock Chase are visible as the canal follows the river valley northwards to Stone, another town which once relied heavily on the canal for its trade. We are now nearing the industrial heart of the Trent & Mersey.

The first sight of industry comes in a setting of lovely parkland at Barlaston, where Wedgwood came after abandoning the old works at Etruria. Visitors can see the factory and the excellent

The entrance to Harecastle Tunnel. The water is stained by the minerals from the underground workings.

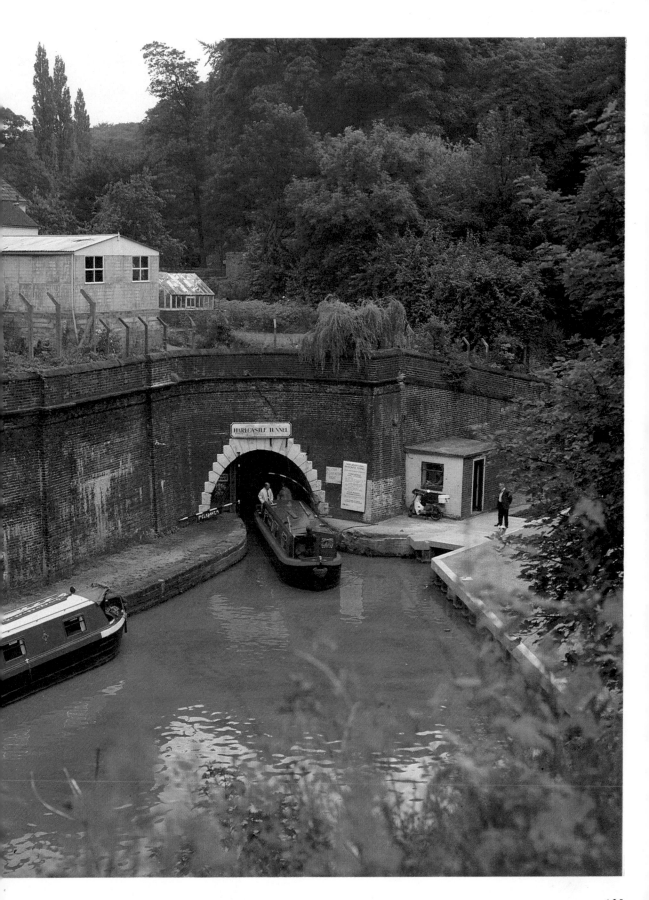

The Trent & Mersey Canal

Wedgwood Museum. Up ahead is Stoke-on-Trent where the potworks still line the canal which climbs up a flight of locks to Etruria and the flint mill stuck into the angle made by the arrival of the Caldon Canal. Beyond that are the sad gaps left by the demolition of the original Wedgwood's works. All that remains are a few small buildings and Wedgwood's much altered house, Etruria Hall. This whole area has changed. Quite recently there was a thrilling passage through the centre of busy Shelton Steelworks, but now Shelton too is dead. The journey through Stoke ends at Harecastle Hill and the two canal tunnels. The tiny Brindley tunnel which cost him so much effort is closed, but the new Telford tunnel remains in use. Traffic, however, is one-way, controlled by the tunnel keeper or at weekends by a system which allows southbound boats in during the morning, northbound in the afternoon.

At the far end, boaters come out to daylight and work as the canal begins to descend from the Etruria summit. The Macclesfield Canal (see p. 98) turns off to cross the main route at the Red Bull locks. This leads on to an area of rolling country which lasts up to the approach to Middlewich. This is a region dominated by salt works and salt mines, where subsidence has had a marked effect on the land. Middlewich itself, with its junction with the Shropshire Union (see p. 110), also marks the reappearance of wide locks, but wide boats can no longer use the waterway since the old broad aqueduct at Croxton was replaced by a narrow version. The last few miles are scenically among the finest on the route as the salt flashes, the ponds formed by mining subsidence, are left behind for a high passage along the rim of the Weaver valley. At Anderton, (see p. 108) there is a turning off for the lift down to the Weaver while ahead the hills are pierced by two somewhat crooked tunnels, Saltersford and Preston Brook. At the end of the latter tunnel, the Trent & Mersey officially stops and becomes the Bridgewater Canal, (see p. 96). It seems almost an anticlimax to reach the end of such a memorable journey to find nothing but a tiny signpost in a quiet cutting, but perhaps it is all in keeping with the unassuming but very real pleasures offered by the Trent & Mersey Canal.

A traditional narrow boat squeezing through the bridge at Fradley Top Lock.

The Caldon Canal

It seems incredible that such a short canal, a mere 17½ miles, can offer so much – such variety, such interest and such superb scenery. It begins with the sharp turn from the Trent & Mersey at Etruria, climbing at once through a two-lock staircase to swing round past Hanley Park and a number of potworks on a far from straight course. This is true potteries country which it would be a shame to leave were it not for the promise of such fine countryside ahead, which the canal wriggles through via some decidedly sharp bends.

At Hazelhurst Junction the way divides. The main line falls through three locks, while the Leek Branch keeps to a high level, crossing the main line on a handsome aqueduct to end at a basin on the edge of town. The main line joins the Churnet valley at Cheddleton. Here are to be found a pair of water-mills with all their machinery intact and working, which were used not for grinding corn but for crushing flint for the potworks of Stoke. The kilns where the flints were heated at the start of the process are built into the canal wharf. Meanwhile, the scenery just goes on getting better and better. The canal runs directly into the Churnet and the river is followed for a mile to Consall Forge, a spot which can also boast one of the canal system's most remote pubs. The climax of the whole trip comes with the final three miles down the outstandingly beautiful river valley to Froghall. At the very end is low, narrow Froghall Tunnel where many a boat has left its paintwork and occasionally its woodwork as well. Most prefer to stop and walk the last few yards to the terminus with its warehouse and giant lime kilns. Froghall Basin is both a beautiful spot and an industrial archaeologist's paradise, characteristics which are shared by the whole of this splendid canal.

The Grand Union Canal, Leicester Section

Above Cruising on the Welford Arm.

The character of the Leicester section is quite unlike that of the rest of the Grand Union. It is formed by the original Grand Union, a narrow canal linking the Grand Junction to Leicester, and the Soar Navigation. For many, this is the very best of the Grand Union, and certainly the combination of a journey through the heart of rural England and some spectacular canal features is hard to resist.

The Leicester section leaves the Grand Union main line (see p. 51) at Norton Junction at the top of Buckby locks and is soon crossed by two roads, separated in time by about 2000 years. First comes Roman Watling Street, closely followed by the M1 at Watford. Motorway users know this for the Watford Gap service station, but canal users have far more to look forward to. Ahead lies the impressive sight of the Watford staircase, five locks run together, followed by two more, climbing up under the shadow of the motorway. Having got up the locks there is a mile of

twisting waterway before the canal disappears underground for almost a mile in the Crick Tunnel.

Coming out of Crick Tunnel, there are still hills in plenty up ahead, which the canal wanders around, those same hills preventing it from ever actually reaching any of the villages that are glimpsed on the horizon. It is as quiet and remote as a canal can be, though not necessarily promising a trouble free journey as the route is notorious for running short of water in dry summers. A short arm does lead to a pleasant mooring at Welford, but the main route continues its lonely progress through the woods and fields. The battle to circumvent every hill in the region is temporarily abandoned at Husbands Bosworth, where the canal goes through the hill in a second tunnel. But then, on re-emerging it goes right back to its meandering ways until Foxton, where the hills are at last faced full on and the canal leaps down 75 feet by ten locks arranged in two staircases. In 1900, engineers decided to bypass the

locks by means of an inclined plane. Rails were laid on the side of the hill, on which ran two caissons, wheeled boxes full of water, each large enough to float two narrow boats. They were counterbalanced, so that the ascending caisson was lifted by the weight of its descending partner. It reduced the time needed to climb the hill but it was not a success and was finally broken up in 1928. Now, however, restorers are planning to rebuild the entire plane.

At the bottom of the locks, boats can turn right for a pleasant four-mile run to equally pleasant Market Harborough, or turn left to continue on towards Leicester. The countryside remains peaceful and hilly, and the canal continues to squirm through to Saddington Tunnel. More locks continue the descent, though not in the spectacular fashion of Foxton, as the canal briefly abandons its lonely route by actually calling in at the village of Newton Harcourt. It has a few more miles to go before the loneliness is finally dispelled by the suburbs of Leicester. There is a wide sweep round Glen Parva as the canal turns to run right alongside the River Soar, which it will soon join to become the Soar Navigation. The passage through the city is an exciting one, running past some remarkably handsome cotton mills and Abbey Park, where the old Abbey pumping station with its vast steam engine is home to the Museum of Technology.

At Belgrave Lock, the canal is abandoned for the waters of the river which turns out, if anything, to be marginally less tortuous than the artificial canal. However, where the canal is notorious for water shortages, the Soar is equally well known for flooding, a problem which a river improvement scheme put forward in 1982 is designed to remedy. Assuming one has missed the floods, a trip down the Soar is a most enjoyable experience, the route being largely through peaceful countryside, the way marked by a mixture of hills and meadows. Not surprisingly, the river does actually reach villages including pretty Barrow-on-Soar and it also passes through Loughborough, home of the Great Central Railway with its old steam trains. There is little change in the scenery beyond Loughborough, and who would want it, though the mighty towers of Ratcliffe power station are visible for many a mile. They mark the end of the line and the last lock before the waters of the Soar flow on to join those of the Trent (see p. 77). The lock itself is a model of trim lawns and smart paint, a last pleasantry to end this most attractive of routes.

Below Foxton locks.

The Erewash

This very industrial canal does not have a great deal of traffic on it. Perhaps the prospect of 15 locks in 12 miles past old ironworks to a dead end does not seem especially enticing. Add to this the problems of rubbish and vandalism that affect all little-used waterways and one might wonder why it is travelled at all. Certainly no one can pretend that this is a pretty canal but it does have many interesting features and for those with an interest in industrial history it is a veritable treasure chest.

The canal leaves the Trent (see p. 77)

at Trent Lock by the big Navigation Inn and soon reaches Long Eaton with its long, low, nineteenth-century lace factories. Although the route is largely urban, there are wide views across the countryside of the Erewash valley. The massive Stanton ironworks which once provided so much trade for the canal is now a gaunt ruin on the edge of Ilkeston. Beyond that is open country again looking over to the colliery town of Eastwood where D.H. Lawrence was born. Thanks to local restorers, the route ends in a fine wide basin at Langley Mill.

The great Northern Basin. The junction of the Erewash, the disused Nottingham and the Cromford Canals.

The Cromford Canal

At present little more than a mile of canal is in water, and if restored as planned it will still be only three miles long with no connection to other waterways. Yet the effort is worth while, for the canal is unique. It was built to join the cotton mills of Cromford, the first of their kind in the world, to the Erewash. At the Cromford end, close by the original mill, is the old wharf and canal museum and here one can take a horse-drawn boat trip along the lovely Derwent valley to Leawood. Here an abundance of riches can be found. First there is the junction with the Cromford & High Peak Railway which led over the hills to the Peak Forest Canal. Then there is a fine aqueduct and alongside it the Leawood pumping station with a splendid preserved beam engine. Restorers are now at work extending the navigation further down the valley.

Leawood Pumping Station. One of the problems facing engineers in the nineteenth century was that of water supply. At Leawood, the water was pumped up to the canal by steam engine. The original 1849 engine has been restored to working order.

The South-West

The region is quite unlike any of the others we have looked at so far, in that the canals and rivers are widely spread, few of them being navigable throughout their length. One waterway, the Kennet & Avon, could be described as the major restoration project in Britain. It is certainly the longest-running project, for work began in 1962 and the first 20 years ended with much achieved – but much still to do. The same is true to greater and lesser degrees with other waterways in the region. The Thames & Severn restoration is only at the beginning of what promises to be a difficult but rewarding task. The Brecon & Abergavenny Canal, on the other hand, is a spectacularly successful waterway and the question now being asked is how much further it can be extended. In other regions there has seemed to be some sort of unifying theme but here all is diversity and there are some true canal oddities to be found. Our survey begins with a canal that has remained in continuous use ever since it was built, Britain's first ship canal, the Gloucester & Sharpness.

The Gloucester & Sharpness Canal

The Stroudwater and the Thames & Severn Canals

The Kennet & Avon Canal

The Brecon & Abergavenny Canal

The Exeter Ship Canal

The Bude Canal

The Tamar and the Tavistock Canal

The Bridgwater & Taunton Canal

The Grand Western Canal

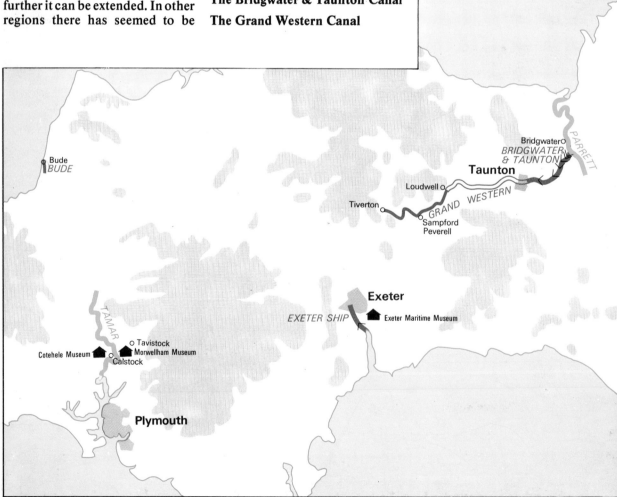

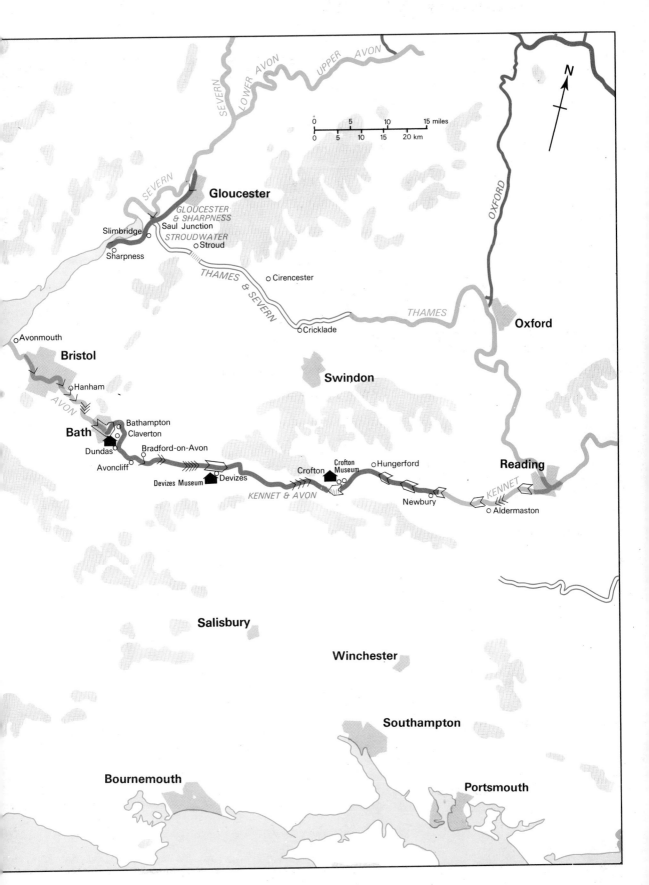

N

| SEVERN | LOWER AVON | UPPER AVON |

OXFORD

SEVERN

Gloucester

GLOUCESTER & SHARPNESS

Saul Junction

STROUDWATER

Slimbridge

Sharpness

Stroud

Cirencester

THAMES & SEVERN

Cricklade

THAMES

Oxford

Avonmouth

Bristol

Hanham

AVON

Swindon

Bath

Bathampton
Claverton

Dundas

Avoncliff

Bradford-on-Avon

Devizes Museum

Devizes

Crofton
Crofton
Museum

Hungerford

Newbury

KENNET & AVON

Aldermaston

Reading

KENNET

0   5   10   15 miles
0   5   10   15   20 km

Salisbury

Winchester

Southampton

Bournemouth

Portsmouth

The Gloucester & Sharpness Canal

This was originally known as the Gloucester & Berkeley Canal, designed to take seagoing vessels from the Severn to Gloucester. This was achieved, but the Severn link was made slightly higher up at Sharpness Point. The canal continues to carry commercial traffic, and pleasure cruisers need to take care and remember that this is a busy navigation on which traffic movement is strictly controlled. Obviously, being a ship canal, it is wide and mostly straight, passing through the flat lands of the Severn plain. It does, however, offer some interesting features. The bridges are all low swing bridges, controlled by bridge keepers from their charming cottages with slightly incongruous classical porticos. It is an excellent route for bird watchers as it runs close to the Slimbridge Wild Fowl Trust. The main interest, however, lies in the docks at either end, both Sharpness and Gloucester offering splendid examples of nineteenth-century dock architecture, the latter being outstanding, as the entire basin is ringed by tall warehouses.

At Gloucester boats can lock down into the Severn (see p. 116), and vessels can also join the tidal river at Sharpness, for the journey to Bristol, but this should not be attempted by the novice. There is one junction, a waterways crossroads at Saul which, if the Stroudwater and Thames & Severn Canal Trust have their way will one day be busy again since restoration is now under way.

Below Gloucester Docks.

The Stroudwater and the Thames & Severn Canals

The two waterways can most conveniently be treated as one, since they form a continuous line, linking the Thames to the Severn: or, one should say, did form such a line, for they have long been derelict and in places have all but disappeared. The Trust who have started on the restoration are hoping to see the job completed by the year 2000, so there is no great rush to book your hire boat. It is, however, a very exciting project, for the canal runs through some of the most beautiful parts of the Cotswold countryside.

With navigation still a distant prospect, this will be little more than the briefest glimpse at the canal. At Saul, a short arm runs down to the Severn, while the main route heads off towards Stroud, along a route lined with woollen mills. More mills are to be found on the far side of the town, many of them very old. Chalford Mill, for example, once belonged to Corpus Christi College, Oxford, and dates back to the sixteenth century. Next to it is one of the tiny circular lock cottages, typical of the Thames & Severn. Beyond this is

beautiful Golden Valley, leading to Sapperton Tunnel, the classical eastern portico of which has been restored. The canal continues eastward to Cirencester, though sections have almost completely disappeared from view. It is too soon to say when or even if the whole canal will be restored, for there are many engineering and political problems still to be overcome.

Below The restored portico of Sapperton Tunnel at Coates.

The Kennet & Avon Canal

This is a major waterway in every sense of the phrase. It runs from Reading to Bristol, a course of almost 90 miles, with 106 wide locks, two mighty aqueducts and a tunnel. It has some quite magnificent scenery, passes through the most elegant city in Britain and has two pumping stations of great historical interest. Given all these factors it is not so difficult to see why after more than 20 years of effort, the Kennet & Avon Canal Trust are still cheerfully pushing on with their restoration programme.

The Kennet & Avon consists of three quite distinct sections. The first, and earliest, is the navigation based on the River Kennet between Reading and Newbury. This is followed by a purely artificial waterway to Bath, where it joins the Avon Navigation which officially ends at Hanham on the outskirts of Bristol. From here, the Avon comes under the jurisdiction of the Bristol City Council and continues to Bristol docks and the Severn at Avonmouth. Already, considerable portions of the system are in use, but most craft are limited to the two extremities where there is access from other parts of the waterways system. Boats can use part of the Kennet from Reading, and from the Severn at Avonmouth there is a considerable length open, extending, at the time of writing, to Dundas on the far side of Bath. As the situation is constantly changing and developing, the canal will be treated in the following description without any reference to the current state of navigation.

Those who enter the Kennet at Reading get little hint of the true character of the waterway, for the entrance is right next to the gasworks and looks like a turn into a drab little side street after travelling the Thames main road. Once through the first lock, operated by the Thames Conservancy, the navigation continues on a very intimate, back-street sort of route, with a number of alarmingly sharp bends. This being a river navigation, locks are accompanied by weirs, so caution is necessary. Once the town has been left behind, the route becomes very much one of the open countryside, a character which it will retain through most of its length. The older locks on the Kennet are of a curious construction, with sloping turf sides, several of which have already been replaced by more conventional locks. Soon the route is joined by the railway, the old Great Western line, which will remain as a faithful

companion for most of the way. Another recurring feature of the Kennet is the swing bridge, which helps to keep the crew busy.

The journey to Newbury is marked by a steady alternation of river and artificial cutting through woods and fields, with the occasional village, such as Aldermaston, perhaps better known to walkers than to boaters. The approach to Newbury is past the race course, but it is the passage through the town centre which is most rewarding. Kennet wharf, its old stone warehouse a lonely reminder of trading days, is followed by

the narrow opening of the old balustraded bridge in the town centre. Beyond that it opens out into as splendid a river scene as one could wish to see, with mills, church and old terraces facing the water.

The artificial canal now takes over, but continues to follow the wooded Kennet valley on a quiet route, dotted by water-mills, to Hungerford. This is another very attractive town, with a broad main street, but the canal passes along the edge to head off on a gently climbing path through rolling countryside, to Crofton. Here a flight of locks leads up

to the summit level, and at the bottom is a lake, Wilton Water. The engineer John Rennie needed the lake water to keep the summit level supplied, so he built a pumping station to lift the water to the top of the flight. It is still there, a large brick building with two beam engines inside; the older of the two, a Boulton and Watt engine of 1812, is the oldest steam engine in the world still able to perform its original task. Crofton on working days is a place of pilgrimage for all steam enthusiasts.

The canal passes through Bruce Tunnel to emerge into a wooded cutting which marks the end of the short summit with the first of many locks that will lead down to the Avon valley. But for the present there are just four locks before the 15-mile-long Wiltshire pound. This is perhaps the quietest, most peaceful section on the whole canal, passing through the undulating country by cutting and embankment. Even the railway temporarily deserts the scene. A few villages creep close to the water as welcome visitors, and what a pleasure it is to find that, for once, when expectations are aroused by a name as mellifluous as Honey Street, those expec-

Above Robert Adam's Pulteney Bridge crosses the Avon at Bath.

Left above A misty morning on the river at Wootton.

Left below A restored lock at Seend Cleeve.

The Kennet & Avon Canal

tations are met in full. This gentle idyll ends very abruptly at Devizes. Not that the town is other than pleasant – but gentleness is certainly not the word for the Devizes flight. The 29 broad locks, with side ponds terraced into the hill to act as mini-reservoirs, go charging down the hill and, as they are mostly set in a straight line, they make a truly awesome sight.

After Devizes, the canal returns to normality with another pleasant rural meander to Semington and the junction with the derelict Wilts & Berks Canal, parts of which are being restored. The Kennet & Avon continues on to pass above the ancient wool town of Bradford-on-Avon, one of the popular beauty spots of the area. The town itself is built on the steep slopes above the river crossing, and the canal too will soon be crossing that same river. At Avoncliff, there is a sharp bend as the canal strides over the Avon on a handsome aqueduct that would be the pride of the Kennet & Avon were it not for the even finer crossing up ahead.

The canal now follows a beautiful route through the trees of the north bank of the river, until the lie of the land forces it back towards the south. This time the crossing is on the Dundas aqueduct, elegantly balustraded and built from the lovely, rich, honey-coloured Bath stone. At the far end is the junction with the Somerset Coal Canal, for which there are also restoration plans. Meanwhile, the Avon valley remains narrow and wooded to Claverton and the second intriguing pumping station. Again, Rennie was faced with the problem of having a water supply, in this case the River Avon, below his canal and here he found a most ingenious solution. Why not, he argued, let the river itself do the work? So the pumping station was built with a water-wheel turned by the Avon, working a pump which lifted its waters. As at Crofton, everything is in full working order.

At Bathampton, the valley opens out for the approach to Bath and the canal makes a suitably dignified entrance to the Georgian city. It passes through Sydney Gardens, under fine ornamental bridges, past equally fine Georgian buildings, the canal company's own offices among them. Then it makes its final drop down the Bath flight to the Avon. This was always an exciting trip, but has now been made even more so as locks 8 and 9 have been run together into one deep lock. The river is joined close by Robert Adam's Pulteney Bridge, with its row of shops in the old manner.

The remainder of the journey to Bristol is by the Avon Navigation and is as attractive as the rest of the trip and just as interesting. Along the way are many remains of the old brass industry of the region, easily recognized by their pyramidal furnaces. Below Hanham the river is tidal, but is then left for the artificial cutting which passes between grand warehouses built in a style that became known as Bristol Byzantine. Safe moorings can be found in the dock basins in the heart of the city. It is possible to continue on to Avonmouth and the Severn, but the trip is not to be recommended to the inexperienced. As yet the journey from Reading to Bristol is impossible, but at least one can say that it will be possible in the not too distant future and that will be a day to fly the flags and open the champagne.

Below A section of the balustraded Dundas Aqueduct.

The Brecon & Abergavenny Canal

This is the one navigable canal that remains entirely within Welsh borders, and if Wales is only to be represented by the one canal then it could hardly have chosen a more attractive champion. It lies within the Brecon Beacons National Park and the scenery has all the grandeur that one would expect from the region.

The start at the Brecon end is not what it was. The original terminus is closed, so the canal now simply begins without the benefit of preliminaries and heads out of town along the line of the Usk valley. Those approaching from the opposite direction should be warned that there is no space to turn at the end, and all but short boats that come up to Brecon will find themselves backing out again for half a mile. Beyond the first lock, the canal turns to cross the Usk on the very attractive Brynich aqueduct. It then heads for the hills which are to be such a dominant feature for the rest of the journey. Indeed, of all the canals in Britain which make their way into hilly country, there can surely be none to compare with this for the feeling it gives of intimacy with those hills. Other canals may wind round them or stride through them, but the Brecon seems to be a part of them, its line moulded to the contours of the land.

The canal passes Talybont on an embankment, goes through a short tunnel, winds in typical style around a hill and then climbs five locks to a higher level: and what a lovely tree-shaded flight of locks this is. Now, from its lofty perch, the canal looks down over the Usk valley cradled by hills, and follows its own lonely path. Beautiful little towns such as Crickhowell are scarcely touched but come within walking distance. The village of Gilwern is met, if briefly, beneath the shadow of aqueduct and embankment. The scenery is now increasingly dominated by the rising bulk of the Blorenge, a wooded hill which the canal skirts at a high level. At Llanfoist, there is a fascinating interchange, where the old tramroad or horse-drawn railway joins the canal. Any trip on the Brecon Canal can be enlivened by exploration of the old tramways that linked it to the industries of South Wales.

The route follows the contour of the hill, forced into extravagant curves by the lie of the land and offering superb views across the valley. Eventually it twists its way to Pontymoile on the outskirts of Pontypool where the Brecon & Abergavenny continues for half a mile to the old Monmouthshire Canal. Few who travel this way can feel anything but regret that this most spectacularly beautiful of passages is all but over, but they can take comfort from the thought that plans are afoot for extending navigation another two miles to Pontnewydd. If one were to stick one's neck out and answer that so frequently repeated question – which is the best canal to introduce beginners to the delights of inland waterways? – then this could well be the choice.

Above A typical stone bridge on the Brecon canal.

Below Llanfoist.

The Exeter Ship Canal/The Bude Canal

The Exeter Ship Canal

This canal is assured of a place in the history books, for it had the first pound lock in Britain. It has changed considerably over the centuries, but still fulfils the same basic function of providing Exeter with access to the sea. A ship canal, with just two locks in five miles, it is little used nowadays. Once, however, it helped the development of Exeter into an important port, and there is ample evidence of that importance in the docks, warehouses and rather grand Customs House in the city. These now provide an altogether appropriate setting for the Exeter Maritime Museum, where the exhibits include a steam dredger designed by Isambard Brunel for the docks at Bridgwater, and a number of historical craft displayed afloat.

Below The sea lock at Bude.

The Bude Canal

This is unlike other canals in this book in that it is scarcely navigable at all. It is included because it is of outstanding interest and makes a fascinating object for exploration. Cornwall is not so well endowed with canals that one can afford to overlook a route as interesting as this, even if exploration does involve a good deal more walking than boating.

Originally the canal ran inland from Bude for 35½ miles, but is now reduced to a little over a mile and just one lock. Still, even that short length has much to offer, for how many other canals start on the seashore? That is what the Bude Canal does, pushing itself out across the beach to the sea, the lock allowing boats to pass between sea and canal. Not that the canal was intended for conventional boats at all, for on its inland journey it was soon faced by high hills, which could never have been surmounted by

conventional means. So, the Bude Canal was built as a tub-boat canal, the boats being simply iron tubs with wheels at the bottom which could be towed along the waterway. When the hill was reached, they were floated along to an inclined plane with a railed track, up which they could be hauled. An example of one of these tub-boats can be seen in the museum housed in the wharf warehouse at Bude.

It is still possible to follow the line of the Bude Canal as far as the great inclined plane on Hobbacott Down, 900 feet long and abandoned for many years. This, and other planes, lifted the tub-boats to a terminus at the great reservoir now known as Tamar Lake, 450 feet above sea level. The whole canal was an engineering triumph, but only worked for 70 years before being closed down in the 1890s. The town itself remains an attractive seaside resort set well back from the sands.

The Tamar and the Tavistock Canal

The River Tamar, which forms the boundary between Devon and Cornwall has been navigable for centuries and, in the days when the banks were lined with copper mines and lime kilns, it was a major trading route. It remains navigable from Plymouth all the way inland to Weir Head, where a derelict lock bars progress. The river is tidal throughout and thus requires caution.

The lower reaches round Plymouth are the busiest, and here the river is crossed by the last great work of Brunel, the Royal Albert railway bridge, still carrying trains on the main line from London to Penzance. The river soon begins to narrow in, however, as it carves vast sweeping bends to reach the wharf at Cotehele. This area, property of the National Trust, has been extensively developed to show the old life of the Tamar as a working river. All round the wharf are the lime kilns which provided cargo. The little warehouse is now a maritime museum, alongside which is a fully rigged Tamar sailing barge. Another bend beneath the high cliffs brings Calstock, once a thriving port, deriving its trade from the mines whose engine house chimneys can still be seen. All that is gone, but the tall concrete viaduct still carries trains across the river.

Another three miles of travel brings vessels to Morwellham, once a port that surpassed Calstock, and now home to an industrial museum. There is ample evidence of the old days in the extensive quays and warehouses, and one can trace the line of the inclined plane that leads up the hill to the Tavistock Canal. A short length of the canal can be followed to the point where it disappears into an incredibly narrow tunnel opening. The canal is unnavigable, though it has left behind some fine buildings, notably the warehouses at the Tavistock end.

Below Tavistock Canal Tunnel.

The Bridgwater & Taunton Canal/The Grand Western Canal

The Bridgwater & Taunton Canal

The canal was built to link Taunton to Bridgwater and from there via the River Parrett to the sea. Some restoration work has already been undertaken, and it is hoped that all will one day be restored. But, as with the rest of the waterways of the South-West, it is short and isolated and will be serving a mainly local interest. Not that this in any way invalidates restoration plans, for it is a most attractive waterway running through a popular holiday area. And it has something very special to offer in Bridgwater, a busy port throughout the seventeenth and eighteenth centuries, where many of the old buildings survive in the dock area.

The Grand Western Canal

The Grand Western scarcely lives up to its name, being just under 11 miles of lock-free canal. It is, in fact, one of those many schemes of the canal age which never achieved their objectives. It was meant to join the Bristol and English Channels, but there it sits in the middle of Somerset reaching neither. It runs from Tiverton to Loudwells, a quite blissfully peaceful canal set in equally tranquil country. Though it is interesting to note, in passing, that during the construction of the canal, the scene was far from peaceful. The navvies rioted at Sampford Peverell, and when it was all over there was one dead and many injured. That is long forgotten, and the canal now retains its peace by a ban on powered craft. Those who visit here paddle, or, if less energetic, take a trip on the horse-drawn passenger boat.

Originally, the Grand Western was joined to the Bridgwater & Taunton by a tub-boat canal, and the true enthusiasts can follow the footpath along the old, long-disused link.

Right The Albert Street cutting on the Bridgwater.

Scotland

The country has few waterways which, given its geography, is scarcely surprising. There were once rather more than can be seen today, but of its four surviving canals, only two are in regular use. The Scots can, however, claim with some justification that though they have little, what they do have is of the very highest quality.

The Union Canal

The Forth & Clyde Canal

The Crinan Canal

Loch Lomond

The Caledonian Canal

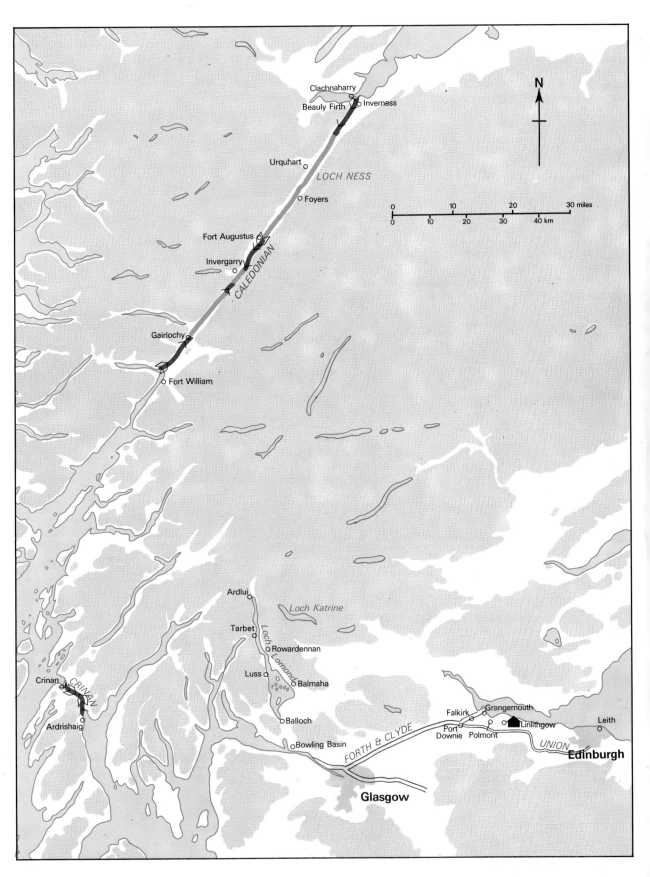

N

Clachnaharry
Beauly Firth
Inverness

Urquhart

LOCH NESS

Foyers

Fort Augustus

Invergarry

CALEDONIAN

Gairlochy

Fort William

0   10   20   30 miles
0   10   20   30   40 km

Ardlui

Loch Katrine

Tarbet

Rowardennan

Loch Lomond

Luss

Balmaha

Crinan

CRINAN

Ardrishaig

Balloch

Falkirk
Grangemouth

Port
Downie   Polmont

Linlithgow

Leith

Bowling Basin

FORTH & CLYDE

UNION

Edinburgh

Glasgow

The Union Canal

The full title, the Edinburgh & Glasgow Union Canal, tells you precisely the function this canal was intended to fulfil, but which, alas, it fulfils no longer. Originally, it connected with the Forth & Clyde Canal (see p. 158) via a flight of 11 locks at Falkirk, after which it ran lock free to Edinburgh. Those locks were closed in 1933 and the rest of the canal in 1965, since when navigation has been blocked by road developments. Sections remain usable and indeed are used, but the long-term aim of restoration of the whole waterway is still some way from realization.

The old start of the canal at Port Downie near Falkirk is still marked by the pub, The Union, but the canal itself now starts 100 feet up the hill and after only a mile disappears into the 696-yard-long Falkirk Tunnel. It re-emerges into a deep cutting spanned by the high 'laughin' and greetin' bridge', so called because of the faces, one happy, one

glum, carved in the keystones. They are said to represent the two contractors who worked on the canal, one of whom made a fortune while the other went bankrupt. As the canal leaves Falkirk there is a short breathing space before Polmont and then comes rather more open countryside and an unusual basin. The Union had a busy passenger trade, but here they left the boat to continue by rail. A little further along is the first of three mighty aqueducts that are the main attractions of this canal. All are stone built, with a cast-iron lining to the trough. This, across the Avon, is the largest, rising 86 feet above the river. It is over 800 feet long and is carried on 12 arches. At the far end is another reminder of passenger boat days in the extensive stable block.

Linlithgow is an attractive town and a busy canal centre with a museum and trip boat. The scenery continues to be fine, and when industry appears in the

aromatic form of a distillery it is not unwelcome. The second of the big aqueducts, across the Almond, is almost as grand as the first and gives equally spectacular views across the wooded valley. The last of the aqueducts, at Slateford, is very different. It crosses the Water of Leith within Edinburgh itself. The canal ends abruptly, the last section having been filled in. The old basin is just a memory, but a memory perpetuated in an inscription on the cinema in Lothian Road. We must now hope that navigation on the Union Canal will not always be just a memory as well.

Below The splendid Almond Aqueduct.

Right The canal at Ratho.

The Forth & Clyde Canal/The Crinan Canal

The Forth & Clyde Canal

This, the first canal project in Scotland, has suffered a fate similar to the Union Canal. It was closed in 1962, not because there was anything wrong with it but because it got in the way of road construction. So, the canal which cut right across southern Scotland, linking east coast to west, was lost and a once busy route is steadily falling into decay. Not that matters are being allowed to rest there, for there is a vigorous movement in favour of restoration. It is a movement with wider backing than many, for the canal would be usable by seagoing vessels as well as by ordinary canal cruisers. Bridges are the major problem in the way of restoration, for the canal was designed to take tall masted vessels and all bridges were made movable. Several are now all too unmovable. Given the will on the part of officialdom, however, restoration would definitely be feasible.

The canal begins at Bowling Basin, which is used as a non-tidal mooring for vessels on the Clyde. The canal itself comes as something of a surprise. Begun in what the English think of as the Brindley age, it has quite different characteristics with broad locks, embankments, bascule bridges, a fine four-arched aqueduct across the Kelvin and several smaller aqueducts. The first part of the canal runs past the famous Clydebank shipyards to a branch leading down towards Glasgow and terminating at Port Dundas, where the company built themselves remarkably handsome offices. The main line has some very pleasant scenery, especially on its long summit level from near the junction with the Glasgow branch, to Windford where the descent into Falkirk begins. The canal in the town has been landscaped and it runs past the impressive Rosebank distillery with its even more impressive bonded warehouse, built on a triangular site between road and canal. The route ends at Grangemouth docks, built in the nineteenth century. Even if the canal were not as interesting as it, in fact, is, its opening would be very welcome to the many yachtsmen who now have to travel to northern Scotland and the Caledonian Canal if they wish to cross from coast to coast. A reopened Forth & Clyde would save them hundreds of miles.

The Crinan Canal

This canal offers a nine-mile artificial cutting as an alternative to the 130 mile-long trip round the Mull of Kintyre, and a remarkably pleasant alternative it is too. The southern end of the canal is at Ardrishaig on Loch Gilp, which is a short arm leading off Loch Fyne. Here, beyond the shelter of the little stone harbour, is the sea lock, the first of eight to lift the canal to its summit. The scenery along the way is very typical of the West Highlands with the canal passing between heather-covered hills. The summit is less than a mile long, leading to the first of seven locks which take the canal down to the shore of Loch Crinan. This is the most dramatic part of the canal, as it carves through the rocks to end at the lovely little Crinan harbour with its splendid view towards the Western Isles.

Below Bowling Basin, Glasgow, on the Forth & Clyde Canal.

Right The Crinan Canal.

Loch Lomond

The one thing everybody knows about Loch Lomond is that its banks and braes are indisputably bonny. The other thing that summer tourists rapidly discover is that the main road along the western flank is narrow, twisting and one continuous traffic jam. So those who actually want to see the best of the famous beauty spot can either pull on their walking boots and tramp to the 3192-feet summit of Ben Lomond on the eastern shore or take to the water. Trip boats run on the loch, including the handsome paddle steamer *Maid of the Loch*, and there are boats to be hired and slipways for trailed craft. There is a good deal to be seen and enjoyed for the loch is 24 miles long, widening to five miles at the southern end, while the many islands large and small offer a variety of channels to explore.

The largest lochside town is Balloch, starting point for boat trips, but the least attractive spot on the lake. Ahead lies the island of Inchmurrin and ruined Lennox Castle. There are a number of attractive villages on both shores: Luss on the west bank for example and Balmaha on the east, the latter looking across to the island of Inchcailleoch. The eastern shore is dominated by the great Queen Elizabeth Forest Park, and those with a taste for exercise can land at Rowardennan for the track to Ben Lomond. Tarbet marks a road junction where a mere two miles separate Loch Lomond from Loch Long which runs down to the Clyde. At its northern end the loch narrows right down past the Inversnaid Hotel and Rob Roy's Cave to Ardlui at the head of the loch.

One other loch deserves special mention, Loch Katrine to the east of Loch Lomond. Because it acts as a water supply for Glasgow, pleasure boats are barred, but there is a trip boat, the steamer *Sir Walter Scott*, built in 1899. This elegant old lady with her quiet engines does little to disturb the serenity of this beautiful lake.

Below View of Loch Lomond from Balloch.

The Caledonian Canal

The Scots may not have many canals to boast about, but in the Caledonian they have the most majestic of them all, with its unique combination of monumental canal features and superb Highland scenery. As with the Crinan, it was built as a ship canal, this time to save an even longer sea passage – the often dangerous route around the north of Scotland. It was an engineering triumph, but a financial flop. Nevertheless, it remains a busy waterway, still used by fishing boats and increasingly used by pleasure craft, both yachts making a through passage and hire boats specifically designed for use on the canal. The latter are a mixture of motor yachts and cruisers, both of which need to be seaworthy, for the canal runs into Loch Ness where the water can be decidedly rough.

A canal that starts under the shadow of Britain's highest mountain needs to be rather special if it is to make any impression at all on the landscape, and the Caledonian proves equal to the challenge. The actual beginning is low key, with a single sea lock providing access to a short cutting which runs under the West Highland railway swing bridge and the main road to Fort William. Beyond that are the Banavie locks, more popularly and more appropriately known as Neptune's Staircase. These eight interconnected locks lift the canal by 64 feet, each lock being capable of taking vessels up to 150 feet long by 30 feet beam. The poet Robert Southey when he came here with his friend the chief engineer of the canal, Thomas Telford, described the staircase as 'the greatest work of art in Britain'. The canal leads away to the two locks of Gairlochy and the first of the natural lakes that form most of the route, Loch Lochy. The loch is long and thin and apart from the point where the river runs down from Loch Arkaig, it is steeply hemmed in by the forested hills.

Above The deep, artificial cutting at Laggan.

At the far end two locks lead up to a section which could be termed the most impressive work of civil engineering in the canal age, the Laggan Cutting. It might not seem so spectacular as, say, Woodseaves Cutting on the Shropshire Union, so obviously deep and narrow. But here, in this contemporary canal, Telford had to cut just as deep, but to ship canal proportions not those of a narrow waterway. When one thinks of when it was built and the primitive equipment available, the remarkable nature of this deep, tree-lined cutting becomes obvious.

The second stretch of natural water, Loch Oich, has perhaps the most beautiful scenery to be found on the entire waterway, and there can be few more attractive anchorages than that in the little bay by the ruins of Invergarry

The Caledonian Canal

Castle. Close by is an extraordinary monument, a pyramid topped with seven severed heads, commemorating the murder of two sons of Chief Macdonnel and their murderers. Those less concerned with the more violent aspects of Highland history can wander through the green fields of the lochside by Invergarry House.

The next canalized section leads to Fort Augustus, where another impressive staircase, this time of five locks, leads down to Loch Ness past the grounds of a monastery. This is the original Fort Augustus, once a garrison, now an abbey and school. The Loch is long and deep, bordered by hills and famous for its monster, though it would be unwise to expect much in the way of sightings. There are, however, still things to see apart from the splendid Highland scenery. At Foyers there is a waterfall, a hydro-electric station, a rather curiously castellated aluminium smelter and an even odder maritime curiosity in the shape of a Humber keel fitted out as a fully rigged ship. Urquhart Bay, overlooked by Urquhart Castle, provides a sheltered mooring which can be decidedly welcome on a rough day.

The final section of the canal leads from the end of the loch to Inverness, a flight of locks passing through this most attractive town to the sea lock at Clachnaharry. Because the shoreline of the Beauly Firth shelves so gently, Telford was forced to extend his canal out into the Forth on an artificial embankment in order to reach deep water. So the canal ends as it began with a major feat of engineering – and the achievement has not gone unrecognized. On the wall of the old canal offices, on the road behind the canal, are inscribed Southey's memorial verses to Telford, beginning:

Telford it was by whose presiding
  mind
The whole great work was planned
  and perfected.

They are not the world's greatest verses, and one cannot help feeling that Telford left behind a far better, far greater memorial to his genius – the Caledonian Canal itself.

Right The staircase of locks at Fort Augustus.

Safety on the water

Canal and river holidays are safe holidays – tens of thousands of people enjoy them every year without serious mishap. But they are not completely safe holidays, nothing which involves boats and water ever can be. Nevertheless, it is true to say that the great majority of accidents could and should be avoided, and if something does go really amiss then the results can be serious or even fatal. The greatest ally in avoiding serious accidents is common sense, but a few simple rules regularly adhered to can help to reduce risks to a minimum.

The right boat for the journey

It is most important to choose the right kind of craft for the route you have chosen. For canals, the steel-hulled narrow boat is probably best, but for fast-running rivers a deep-keeled boat has advantages. Again, for waterways which link canals and open waters something more sea-worthy is required. Detailed information about choosing your boat is given in 'Using the Waterways'.

Sailing your boat

The first thing to remember is that although your boat may be slow it is also very heavy, so that it carries considerable momentum. Run into an immovable object and the shock of impact can be enormous, quite enough to knock someone off the cabin roof or an unguarded stern or bow and it can be particularly dangerous for anyone walking around the boat.

Care must be taken with steering until you have mastered the art – the basics are quite straightforward, but some of the finer points take practice. Maximum speed is four miles per hour, but REMEMBER you must never go at maximum speed in shallow water and where there are locks and bridges.

Clothing

All members of your party who cannot swim should wear life jackets, and never mind about feeling silly. You will feel a good deal sillier as you go down for the third time.

Always wear proper boating shoes which will help avoid a slip both on the boat and at the locks.

Locks

The various types of locks and the way they work are described in 'Using the Waterways', but it is worth repeating some of the main points as locks can represent danger points on both canals and rivers.

1. **SLOW DOWN when approaching a lock**
2. **NEVER tie up a boat near a lock**
3. **NEVER get too near the back of a lock when you are inside it**
4. **NEVER allow children to run around a lock. One slip in the water could prove fatal, for vicious currents are set up in a lock – strong enough to pull a boat against the full thrust of the engine.**
The golden rule is to be purposeful but steady.

Bridges

Once you have mastered the basic steering skills, bridges should present few problems. Canal bridges have comparatively narrow openings, though there is of course, plenty of room. SLOW DOWN AND LINE UP the boat well in advance. On rivers, by contrast, the arches seem enormous, but caution is needed as the current around a bridge can be tricky.

Mooring

Check possible mooring sites carefully as suitable places can be in short supply. DO NOT leap ashore clutching mooring lines – this can prove very dangerous. Keep mooring lines coiled carefully on board – it is difficult to throw a tangled line to shore, and an untidy deck can lead to accidents. Before setting out ALWAYS check that the mooring spikes and lines are back on board.

General Safety

It is not possible to anticipate every hazard on the waterways, but by taking things calmly and by bearing in mind that many of the objects you meet along the way – lock gates, swing bridges and so on – are like boats, massive and once started cannot easily be stopped, the worst dangers can be avoided.

Never let hands and legs dangle over the side of the boat, particularly in locks and tunnels or anywhere near other craft. That same force that can knock the unwary off the boat can be brought to bear on anything else that gets in the way, including portions of the human anatomy.

REMEMBER – low bridges and human heads make an unhappy combination.

Rivers

TIDAL WATERS SHOULD NEVER BE TACKLED BY THE INEXPERIENCED.

Tidal rivers and commercial waterways present their own special problems. The rule about large objects on the move is even more applicable here, where big barges and coasters are encountered. These are not waterways for beginners, but those who do venture must at least know the rules of the road. Give precedence to the larger craft and make sure that you know what both you and they are doing. A special sound code is used to warn of changes of direction and must be memorized:

> One short blast – I am turning to starboard
> Two short blasts – I am turning to port
> Three short blasts – I am going astern
> Four short blasts (an emergency signal) – I am unable to manoeuvre
> Four short blasts followed by two long – I am going about to port
> Five short blasts (this is the one you should never incur). The official description is – I do not consider you are taking sufficient action to avoid me, which can be interpreted as 'What the hell do you think you are doing?'

Theoretically the same signals should be used and understood on all inland waterways, but seldom are.

River locks present an additional hazard in the shape of weirs. Each year it seems someone takes the wrong channel and instead of heading for the calm, controlled descent of the lock, finds himself faced with a headlong rush across the weir, so make sure you have maps, and make sure that you check those maps regularly.

Conclusion

These are by no means the only rules, but follow these and you will not go far wrong. Again, it must be stressed that water holidays are safe. The chances of you having an accident are considerably less than they are when you cross the road.

Canal Restoration

It must be obvious by now that those who travel by canal owe a great deal to the work of the restorers, the great majority of whom have been volunteers. Much has been done already, but work continues on canals and navigations throughout the country, while new plans are constantly appearing for yet more ambitious projects. This brief look at the restoration story will, it is hoped, do two things: it will help the reader to appreciate the immense effort that has gone towards turning derelict canals into popular cruiseways which thousands use without a thought; and it might even convince that same reader that restoration work is a rewarding activity – and fun. If, at the end, the reader then feels like joining in the work then fine, or feels like contributing to the restoration funds, then equally fine.

It is difficult to put any precise date on the beginning of the restoration movement, but two events stand out: the formation of the Inland Waterways Association in 1946, the organization that was to lead so many campaigns; and the start of work on the southern section of the Stratford-upon-Avon Canal in 1961. The great thing about the Stratford scheme was that it succeeded. It proved conclusively that a canal which had been declared terminally ill could in fact be revived and brought back to vigorous life. The canal was purchased by the National Trust and the actual work was controlled by the energetic David Hutchings, who managed a work force consisting of volunteers, Boy Scouts, soldiers and even prisoners from the local gaol. David Hutchings was to go on to direct other schemes in the area

with equal enthusiasm and equal success. By 1970 the restoration movement was well under way, but there was a real danger of energy being dissipated due to a lack of overall control. It was to counteract that danger that the Waterways Recovery Group (W.R.G.) was formed. Under the leadership of Graham Palmer, W.R.G. became a kind of waterways task force, descending as a great army to cope with major schemes. Anything, it seemed, was possible, and the W.R.G. army of amateur navvies marching under their banner emblazoned with the motto 'We Dig Canals' achieved an enormous amount and continues to be an effective force.

It has been obvious for many years now that the will power and enthusiasm of the restorers has grown rather than

Far left Volunteers at work on the Stroudwater Canal.

Left Restoring a lock on the Devizes flight on the Kennet & Avon Canal.

Above A restorer's plaque on the Ashton Canal.

diminished, but that they are not enough on their own. Costs are rising all the time and while some local councils have been tremendously helpful others have seemed not merely uninterested but downright antagonistic. And a new problem has appeared in recent years. It seemed at first that the aim of the movement should be limited to reopening old waterways, but increasingly the problem should now be seen as keeping them going after restoration. But if there are problems ahead, the last decade has shown that there are many who are ready and eager to face them.

Those not involved in the movement often find it somewhat bewildering. Why should all those people give up their spare time to slosh about in the muck as unpaid labourers? The official answer might be that they are doing something of value, opening up a new recreation route that will be enjoyed by thousands. Certainly this is an important element. Just look at all those who get such immense pleasure travelling the Cheshire or Avon Ring, and then think that this would never have been possible without the amateur navvies. There is, however, another factor. It is actually good fun – dirty, tiring fun certainly – but the satisfaction of working with others towards a common goal, and of seeing the work moving steadily forward, has to be experienced to be believed. The restorers work mainly for their own satisfaction and ask for nothing in return. The next time you travel through Marple locks or along the Upper Avon, just remember that you are there because a lot of people stomped around up to their eyes in muck to make it possible.

The principal restoration agency is:

The Inland Waterways Association
114 Regent's Park Road
London NW1 8UQ
Their regular bulletin gives details of all current restoration schemes.

The Waterways Recovery Group is part of the I.W.A. but can be contacted separately:

Waterways Recovery Group
4 Wentworth Court
Wentworth Avenue
London N3 1YD

A list of all canal societies and restoration groups can be found in the *Waterway Users' Companion* published annually by the British Waterways Board.

Places to Visit

The South-East

Dolphin Yard Sailing Barge Museum
Crown Quay
Sittingbourne
Kent

The museum, based on an old maintenance yard, tells the story of the development of the Thames sailing barge.

The Waterways Museum
Stoke Bruerne
nr Towcester
Northants

The museum stands beside the Grand Union locks and is one of the most important of the canal museums in Britain.

The North-East

Nottingham Canal and Industrial Museum
Canal Street
Nottingham

The museum is housed in a warehouse formerly used by the famous canal carrying company, Fellows, Morton & Clayton.

The Canal Story Exhibition
Clock Warehouse
London Road
Shardlow
Derbyshire

This very attractive building, formerly the Trent Corn Mill, houses an exhibition describing the development of canals.

The North-West

Cromford Canal
Derbyshire

The canal terminus houses a small museum from where horse-drawn boat trips travel the canal. These trips lead to the interchange with the Cromford & High Peak Railway and the Leawood pumping station where the beam engine is occasionally steamed.

The Canal Museum
Savile Town Wharf
Mill Street East
Dewsbury
W. Yorkshire

This museum occupies the former stable block of the Calder & Hebble Navigation.

Windermere Steamboat Museum
Rayrigg Road
Windermere
Cumbria

This is a unique collection of Victorian and Edwardian steam launches and other craft associated with the lake.

The West Midlands

The Black Country Museum
Tipton Road
Dudley
W. Midlands

A major industrial museum based on the Dudley Canal complex, and the starting point for Dudley Tunnel boat trips.

The Boat Museum
Dock Yard Road
Ellesmere Port
S. Wirral

This major collection of canal and river craft is housed in the terminal building and docks of the Shropshire Union Canal. The steam engine that powered the dock's hydraulic system is also preserved.

Ironbridge Gorge and Blists Hill Open Air Museum
N. Cossons
Ironbridge
Telford
Shropshire

At the Blists Hill site there is a restored section of the tub-boat canal leading to the great Hay incline which lowered the tubs to Coalport. See also the wharf warehouse.

Llangollen Canal Exhibition
The Wharf
Llangollen
Clwyd

The museum shows the general history of canals and there are horse-drawn boat trips to Pontcysyllte.

The East Midlands

Cheddleton Flint Mill
Leek Road
Cheddleton
Staffordshire

The two working water-powered flint grinding mills were served by the Caldon Canal and a traditional working narrow boat is moored at the wharf.

The South-West

Bude Historical and Folk Exhibition
The Wharf
Bude
Cornwall

The museum is situated just above the sea lock and includes exhibits on the tub-boat canal.

Pumping Station
Claverton
Avon

The water-powered pumping station which lifted water from the river to the Kennet & Avon Canal is open on Sundays from April to October with occasional weekend demonstrations.

Cotehele Quay
nr Calstock
Cornwall

The quay area has been restored by the National Trust with a maritime museum in the warehouse. The Tamar barge *Shamrock* is moored alongside.

Canal Centre
The Wharf
Devizes
Wiltshire

The small museum in the wharf building stands at the top of the famous flight of 29 locks.

The Exeter Maritime Museum
The Quay
Exeter
Devon

Exhibits include ships and boats from all over the world at the terminus of the Exeter Canal.

Crofton Pumping Station
Great Bedwyn
Wiltshire

The pumping station contains two beam engines used to pump water into the Kennet & Avon Canal. It is open Sundays from April to October and there are regular steamings.

Morwellham Quay
nr Tavistock
Devon

The open air museum centres round the wharf on the Tamar and a copper mine. An inclined plane leads up to the Tavistock Canal.

Further Reading

Pontypool
Gwent

The former toll house on the Monmouthshire and the Brecon Canals at Pontymoile is being developed as a small museum.

Scotland

Linlithgow Canal Museum
Manse Road Basin
Linlithgow
Lothian

The story of the Union Canal is told, and pleasure trips given in a replica steam packet boat, *Victoria*.

I have made no attempt to give detailed opening times as these are constantly changing. Would-be visitors should check with the local tourist office or consult one of the standard annual guides such as that published by the Automobile Association or ABC Historic Publications *Museums & Galleries in Great Britain and Ireland*.

There are a number of guides to waterways and hiring facilities which are published annually:
> *The Canals Book,* Link House
> *Inland Waterways Guide to Holiday Hire,* I.W.A/Haymarket
> *The Lazy Man's Guide to Holidays Afloat,* Boat Enquiries

There are also a number of guides describing individual waterways and groups of waterways which are designed for use on a cruise. These include two important groups of books:
> Nicholson's *Ordnance Survey Guides to the Waterways*
> *Waterways World* Guides

The latter are better but incomplete. Other guides to individual canals are also available.

A number of illustrated books show the canal scene past and present, of which the following can be recommended:
> Anthony Burton & Derek Pratt, *Canal*, David & Charles, 1976
> John Gagg, '*Looking at Inland Waterways*', series, J. Gagg
> Robert Harris, *Canals and their Architecture*, Hugh Evelyn, 1969
> Derek Pratt, *Discovering London's Canals*, Shire Publications, 1977
> Derek Pratt, *Southern Inland Waterways*, Ian Allan, 1982
> P.J.G. Ransom, *The Archaeology of Canals*, World's Work, 1979
> Michael E. Ware, *Britain's Lost Waterways* (two vols), Moorland Publications, 1979

The following deal with particular waterways journeys:
> Anthony Burton, *Back Door Britain*, André Deutsch, 1977
> Frederic Doerflinger, *Slow Boat through Pennine Waters*, Wingate, 1971
> L.T.C. Rolt, *Narrow Boat*, Eyre & Spottiswoode, 1972

For more general information, the following can be recommended:
> John Gagg, *The Observers Book of Canals*, 1982
> Hugh McKnight, *The Shell Book of Inland Waterways* (2nd ed.) David & Charles, 1981

Canal history has been extensively covered and the following provide introductions to the subject:
> Anthony Burton, *The Canal Builders* (2nd ed.) David & Charles, 1981
> Charles Hadfield, *British Canals: An Illustrated History* (6th ed.) David & Charles, 1974
> Charles Hadfield, *The Canal Age*, David & Charles, 1968

Canal Specifications

Unless otherwise shown, the maximum dimensions indicate the largest craft that can negotiate the entire waterway. The figures are given in order, length x breadth x draught.

The South-East

The Medway
43 miles, 10 locks
Allington to Maidstone:
186ft x 21ft 6in x 6ft 6in
Maidstone to Tonbridge:
80ft x 18ft 6in x 4ft 6in

The Thames
146 miles from Limehouse, 44 locks
Limehouse to Oxford:
120ft x 17ft 3in x 3ft 9in
Oxford to Lechlade:
109ft x 14ft 9in x 3ft 6in

The Wey
19½ miles, 16 locks
73ft 6in x13ft 10½in x 3ft

The Wey & Arun Junction Canal
23 miles, 26 locks
Unnavigable

The Arun
22 miles, no locks
Approximately 95ft x 10ft x 4ft at high water

The Basingstoke Canal
31 miles to Greywell, 29 locks
Unnavigable
Dimensions when restored:
72ft 6in x 13ft 6in x 3ft 6in

The Grand Union Canal
Brentford to Birmingham: 138 miles, 165 locks
72ft x 14ft x 3ft 6in (beam 12ft 6in at Camp Hill)
Regent's Canal: 8½ miles, 13 locks, including ship lock
80ft x 14ft 6in x 4ft 6in
Paddington Arm: 13¾ miles, no locks
As main line
Slough Arm: 5 miles, no locks
As main line
Aylesbury Arm: 6¼ miles, 16 locks
72ft x 7ft x 3ft
Northampton Arm: 5 miles, 17 locks
72ft x 7ft x 4ft

The Lee
27¾ miles, 22 locks, including ship lock
88ft x 15ft 6in x 4ft 6in

The Stort
13¾ miles, 15 locks
88ft x 13ft x 5ft

The Chelmer & Blackwater Navigation
13¾ miles, 13 locks
60ft x 16ft x 2ft

East Anglia

The Suffolk Stour
23½ miles, 15 locks
Unnavigable

The Broads
Total navigation approximately 130 miles, no locks
No limit

The Great Ouse
75 miles, 16 locks
Bedford to Denver Sluice:
100ft x 10ft 6in x 4ft 6in
Maximum length at Denver Sluice, 70ft

The Cam
14½ miles, 3 locks
100ft x 14ft x 4ft

The Nene
91¾ miles, 38 locks
78ft x 13ft x 4ft

The Middle Level
Total length of navigable drains, approximately 100 miles
For craft passing Whittlesey:
46ft x 11ft x 3ft 6in
Old Bedford River:
40ft x 10ft 9in x 3ft 6in

The North-East

The Welland
24½ miles, 1 lock
90ft x 30ft x 6ft

The Witham
36 miles, 3 locks
78ft x 15ft 2in x 5ft

The Fossdyke Canal
11 miles, 1 lock
75ft x 15ft x 5ft

The Trent
Derwent Mouth to Trent Falls:
93½ miles, 13 locks
82ft 6in x 14ft 8in x 5ft

The Sheffield & South Yorkshire Navigation
43 miles, 29 locks
61ft 6in x 15ft 6in x 6ft

The Aire & Calder Navigation
34 miles, Goole to Leeds, 13 locks
7½ miles Castleford to Wakefield, 4 locks
132ft x 17ft 9in x 8ft

The Ouse (Yorkshire)
62 miles, 3 locks (Naburn twin locks counting as one)
Trent Falls to York:
150ft x 25ft 6in x 8ft 6in
York to Swale Nab:
60ft x 15ft 3in x 4ft

The Ure and the Ripon Canal
9 miles, to Littlethorpe locks, 3 locks
57ft x 14ft 6in x 4ft 9in

The Wharfe
9¼ miles, no locks
Draught 3ft 6in to 5ft 6in, depending on tide

The Derwent
38 miles, 5 locks
Unnavigable

The Ancholme
19 miles, 2 locks
To Harlam Hill Lock:
80ft x 19ft x 5ft
At Harlam Hill Lock:
69ft x 16ft x 5ft

The Hull
20 miles, no locks
Unlimited, draught 5ft

The Driffield Navigation
7 miles, 7 locks
Unnavigable

The Idle
10¼ miles, no locks
Length unlimited, 18ft x 2ft 6in

The Chesterfield Canal
26 miles to Morse Lock, 16 locks
72ft x 6ft 11in x 3ft 3in

The North-West

The Leeds & Liverpool Canal
127 miles, Leeds to Liverpool, 92 locks
Leeds to Wigan: 62ft x 14ft 4in x 3ft 9in
Wigan to Liverpool: 72ft x 14ft 4in x 3ft 9in
Leigh Branch: 7 miles, 2 locks
72ft x 14ft 4in x 3ft 9in
Rufford Branch: 7 miles, 8 locks
62ft x 14ft 3in x 3ft 6in

The Bridgewater Canal
28 miles, Manchester to Runcorn, no locks
72ft x 14ft 9in x 4ft 3in
Leigh Branch: 11 miles, no locks
72ft x 14ft 4in x 3ft 9in

The Rochdale Canal
33 miles, 92 locks
Navigable section: Ducie Street to Castlefield Junction 1 mile, 9 locks
74ft x 14ft 2in x 4ft

The Ashton Canal
7 miles, 18 locks
70ft x 7ft x 3ft 3in

The Peak Forest Canal
15 miles, 16 locks
70ft x 7ft x 3ft 3in

The Macclesfield Canal
26 miles, 13 locks
70ft x 7ft x 3ft 3in

The Huddersfield Canals
Broad Canal: 3¾ miles, 9 locks
57ft 6in x 14ft 2in x 4ft 6in
Narrow Canal: 20½ miles, 74 locks
Unnavigable

The Calder & Hebble Navigation
21½ miles, 39 locks
57ft 6in x 14ft 2in x 5ft

The St Helens Canal
3½ miles navigable, 1 lock
75ft x 18ft 6in x 6ft

The Manchester Ship Canal
36 miles, 5 locks
600ft x 65ft x 28ft

The Lancaster Canal
42½ miles, no locks
Glasson Arm: 3 miles, 7 locks
72ft x 14ft 6 in x 3ft

The West Midlands
The Weaver
20 miles, 5 locks
130ft x 30ft x 10ft
Anderton Lift:
72ft x 14ft 6in x 5ft

The Shropshire Union
66½ miles Autherley to Ellesmere Port,
46 locks
Middlewich Branch: 10 miles, 3 locks
72ft x 6ft 11in x 3ft 4in

The Dee
35 miles, no locks
Draught 3ft

The Llangollen Canal
46 miles, 21 locks
70ft x 7ft x 2ft 6in

The Montgomery Canal
35 miles, 25 locks
Unnavigable

The Severn
42 miles, Stourport to Gloucester, 6 locks
89ft x 18ft 11in x 5ft 9in

The Avon
44 miles, Tewkesbury to Stratford-upon-
Avon, 17 locks
70ft x 13ft 6in x 4ft

The Stratford-upon-Avon Canal
25½ miles, 56 locks
71ft 8in x 7ft x 3ft

The Worcester & Birmingham Canal
30 miles, 58 locks
71ft 6in x 7ft x 4ft

The Staffordshire & Worcestershire Canal
46 miles, 43 locks
72ft x 6ft 9in x 3ft 6in

The East Midlands
The Birmingham Canal Navigations
Main line, 15½ miles, Birmingham to
Aldersley Junction, 24 locks
71ft 6in x 7ft 1½in x 3ft 6in

The Birmingham & Fazeley Canal
15 miles, 38 locks
71ft 6in x 7ft 1½in x 3ft 6in

The Coventry Canal
Fradley to Coventry, 38 miles, 14 locks
72ft x 6ft 10in x 3ft 10in

The Ashby Canal
22 miles, no locks
72ft x 7ft x 3ft 6in

The Oxford Canal
77 miles, 42 locks
72ft x 7ft x 3ft 6in

The Trent & Mersey Canal
93½ miles, 76 locks
72ft x 7ft x 3ft

The Caldon Canal
17½ miles, 18 locks
72ft x 7ft x 3ft

The Erewash
12 miles, 15 locks
72ft x 14ft x 3ft 6in

The Grand Union, Leicester Section
66 miles, Norton Junction to Trent Junction,
59 locks
70ft x 7ft x 3ft 6in

The Cromford Canal
Originally 17 miles, 14 locks
Navigable 1 mile, no locks

The South-West
The Gloucester & Sharpness Canal
17 miles, 2 locks
190ft x 29ft x 10ft

The Stroudwater and the Thames & Severn Canals
38 miles, 40 locks
Unnavigable

The Kennet & Avon Canal
86½ miles, 106 locks
Partially navigable
73ft x 13ft 10in x 3ft 6in

The Brecon & Abergavenny Canal
33 miles, 6 locks
64ft 9in x 9ft 2in x 3ft

The Bridgwater & Taunton Canal
14 miles, 6 locks
Unnavigable

The Grand Western Canal
11 miles, Loudwells to Tiverton, no locks

The Exeter Ship Canal
5 miles, 3 locks
122ft x 25ft x 10ft 6in

The Bude Canal
Navigable 1 mile, 1 lock
85ft x 24ft x 9ft 6in

The Tamar
17½ miles to Morwellham, no locks
Up to 5ft draught at high water

Scotland
The Union Canal
31 miles, no locks
Unnavigable

The Forth & Clyde Canal
35 miles, 39 locks
Unnavigable

The Crinan Canal
9 miles, 15 locks
88ft x 20ft x 9ft 6in

The Caledonian Canal
60½ miles, 29 locks
150ft x 35ft x 13ft 6in

Index

Acknowledgements

All the photographs in the book were taken by **Derek Pratt** with the exception of the ones on the following pages:

Anthony Burton: 53 (below)
British Waterways Board: 13
Derek Pratt, courtesy of the British Waterways Board: 79, 80–1
Radio Times Hulton Picture Library: 8, 11, 12, 16, 17